OPERATION ODESSA

By

David Serero

CONTENTS

FOREWORD

I am deeply honored to present you my new book called OPERATION ODESSA. I heard this incredible story many years ago. The crazy life of a Jewish man from Odessa (Ukraine) who became a Russian mobster, and hustled the Cali Cartel of Pablo Escobar and was arrested by the D.E.A while he was buying a...Soviet submarine to help the Colombian cartel to bring drugs to the United States.

This story will take you to Odessa (Ukraine), New York, Miami, Moscow, Bogota, Panama and many more countries in the craziness of the 1990s...

You'll read this story as a fascinating thriller, which truly deserves to be adapted as a feature film as it combines all the required elements to make it a perfect one.

If you're a fan of the TV series such as Narcos, then this story definitely is for you!

While I certainly do not encourage anyone to do this, I've always been impressed by how life can bring you adventures and put people (good or bad) in your way.

I wish to thank the protagonists of this book and particularly Mr Ludwig Fainberg, from Jewish origins, who was always very creative (With always a lot of comedy!) when it was about saving his life, and used his « chutzpa » to come out of the most complex situations.

I wish to thank my dad, whom I love and adore above all, and all the people who have encouraged me to bring this book to life. I wish to thank Emily Ashley for her help on the book, as well as the proofreaders.

This title is available as an audiobook.

I wish you to enjoy it!

Sincerely,

David Serero

PROLOGUE

Tiller Russell had just arrived at La Joya Prison at the outskirts of Panama. He had never been to a prison, but he had a fair idea of what to expect. He had done his research and felt prepared. After calling his connect, he sat quietly in his rented Honda and waited. It was an old model which he had chosen to suit the occasion. He needed to remain invisible and unmemorable.

His heart was beating too fast and his eyes were glued to his phone as he waited for the call. He remembered fleetingly, how he had ended up in this absurd situation.

Tiller Russell was a US based filmmaker who explored fiction and documentaries about crime by interacting with the underground world and the law enforcement agents equally. He believed in evidence and the elimination of bias. There was no story until both parties had told their parts. He also had the innate ability to spot a good story from a crowd of gibberish. When he received a call from a DEA agent a week ago, he knew he had nailed a big fish.

"I am going to tell you the craziest true crime story you've ever heard," the narc said. The awe that dripped from his voice only fueled Russell's curiosity.

"Tell me about it."

Then the narc launched into the most unbelievable story. It was about a Russian gangster who sold a military submarine to a popular cartel to move drugs between the United States and Canada. Russell sat silently with his phone pressing against his left cheek and listened like his life depended on it.

"Guess what?" the narc asked out of the blue.

"What?"

"He is in a Panamanian prison for drug and human trafficking, he has a Blackberry inside. Do you want his number?" Russell almost peed on himself. He could not believe his luck. By the time, the narc had ended the call, he was hooked. He knew he had to get the story even if it killed him.

Like a lunatic, he made a few calls and jumped on the plane, praying that Panama would not be the last place he saw. He had ten thousand dollars taped to his leg. He was prepared to bribe his way in and out of the prison.

The call finally came, and he was instructed to approach the gate. He watched two guards mumble inexplicable words into their walkie-talkie before facing him. One looked at Russell with contempt, and the scrutiny made his toes itch. By the time the gate had opened for him, Russell's shirt was already drenched in sweat. He was instructed in poor English to get into the back of a military truck and to obey without asking questions.

Russell had been warned that it was difficult to get in, but almost impossible to get out. As the truck moved across the prison yard, Russell peeped through a small hole and watched a few inmates move food supplies across the open field. Another group was carrying items that he could not decipher from such a distance. One of the guards led Russell to the prison building where he met his connect for the first time at the front desk.

"You know you can't just go in. It took me a lot to get you past that gate," the man mentioned casually while implying that it would cost him. Russell did not give it a second thought before surrendering the money he had on him. He wasn't a rookie and knew that the easiest way around was through his pocket. He pulled out five hundred dollars from his stash and slipped it into the guard's palm smoothly. In retrospect, he realized that there was no need to be stealthy about it. That was a common occurrence in prison.

"His cubicle is at the end of the hall. Once you hit the wall it will be on your left."

Russell opened his mouth to ask the man to lead him to the cubicle, but he shut it almost immediately. He did not want to upset anyone until he had left the prison alive. As Russell turned towards the hall, he knew he had made a mistake. He had chosen the oldest clothes that he had found in a store nearby solely for the sake of blending in. Unfortunately, they were too clean to pass for prison wear. So, he made a quick decision on how to get to his interviewee in one piece. Like a man on the run, he sprinted across the hall, while ignoring the jeering remarks that were thrown brashly at him.

"Americano!"

"Bastard!"

"New meat!"

He was very glad to reach the end of the door and even happier as he fell against it while it gave way immediately. Once he looked at the man in the room, he could not hold back his smile. He knew he had hit the movie jackpot. The Russian was seated on a small metal chair with cuffs on his wrist and a cigar between his lips.

"You're the Russell guy aren't you?" the man asked. Russell nodded and sat down. "You look as if life has been good to you."

"It has."

The man laughed. "Back when I was free, I used to be happy. I could buy anything I wanted," he mused. Russell smiled sadly. The man had committed a chain of crimes, but Russell could almost relate to his feeling of loss.

"I like you," hc said unexpectedly. "Why do you even want to make a movie about me?" Russell had answered the question so many times, but he did not want to upset the man without acquiring important information from him.

"I just like to tell people's stories. Yours definitely deserves to see the light."

The Russian dropped his cigar in the ashtray and looked at Russell squarely.

"So what did those police suckers tell you?"

"Just that you stole a military submarine and sold it to the Cali Cartel. How true is it?"

He chuckled. "What do you think?" He sat up and bent towards Russell like a prancing tiger. Russell felt the urge to move back. The man before him did not look scary, but his track record was enough to instill fear in Russell. "Unfortunately, I can't share the story with you. Those crazy people have sworn to kill me if I say a word."

Russell's shoulder slumped. No amount of money could ever waive a death threat like that, and he did not have enough to attempt to strike a deal.

"Not even an overview?" Russell tried although he already knew anything short of a full story was useless to him.

"Sorry son," the Russian said.

"Thank you, sir," Russell said sullenly and stood. As soon as he reached the door, the Russian stopped him.

"Russell?" he turned abruptly. There was a ray of hope in his eyes. "We can still be friends, you know. You can call me Tarzan." Russell walked away silently. He paid another five hundred to get out of the jail safely. This time, he was accompanied by a guard who literally had to beat the inmates with a stick to keep them away from him. When Russell got out of the prison and out of Panama, he put the whole experience behind him.

One morning while he browsed through the morning paper, his phone beeped. He glanced at it and noticed an email from a strange address. Reluctantly he opened it.

'Jailbreak! I'm out. Let's make a movie.'

Tiller Russell's face lit up instantly. He knew it was Tarzan.

CHAPTER 1

Ludwig 'Tarzan 'Fainberg was born on the January 3rd, 1958 in Odessa, Ukrainian SSR, Soviet Union. Tarzan initially worked as dentist. However, there was a surge in the Jewish immigration, he left for Israel alongside other Jews to join the Israeli Navy. When the United States relaxed the immigrant restrictions for Jews, Tarzan moved to America. Numerous Russian criminals released from prisons by the KGB also guised as Jews with fake passports. Everyone entered the country via Brighton Beach in New York. Before long, the place was named Little Odessa and was no longer welcoming or safe for anyone.

When Tarzan first arrived to America, he fell in love instantly. It was the home of opportunity. Absolutely anything could be considered a real job. He could become anyone from a movie star to a gangster to the head of a fan club with pay. In 1981, Tarzan secured his first job as an 'enforcer 'for the Gambino crime family, an American Mafia organization. All he had to do was burn stores. He had a partner whom he committed arsons within Brooklyn. He termed it '*Jewish Lightning.*'

He considered the job as an easy one. He was only required to put a little fire and make himself scarce. When the firemen came, they practically completed the job of trashing the place. They would shatter the windows to let themselves in, destroy any furniture in their way and douse the place with more water than required to quench the fire. In the end, all else would be in ruins and Tarzan's mission would still be accomplished. He loved his job.

Tarzan did not only commit arson as often as his boss required. He also mauled a few people, trashed houses and destroyed property in attempt to send messages across to people who weren't on good terms with the Gambino family. Also, he was contracted to beat up people that did not pay their debts on time. His clients ranged from loan sharks to drug lords to property owners. One time he had a job to uproot some tenants from a certain apartment. They had not paid their rent for three months and the owner of the building was upset.

Tarzan would have preferred to break in, but his client didn't want his windows shattered. He had to find another way into the house which was easier than he had expected. Tarzan only had to help the tenant carry her groceries to be invited in. She was married to a man in his early sixties who reminded him of his father. Tarzan did not care about his gray hair. He had only come to do his job.

"Nice apartment," he said as soon as he entered inside. He walked to the couch purposeful. The woman had assumed that he wanted to sit down. He ripped the couch easily. He did not care that it was already frayed being it was obvious the family couldn't afford their rent. The woman's husband heard her cry and rushed towards the living room.

"Is there are problem here?"

"Definitely," Tarzan said before he landed a punch against his jaw. Tarzan heard it snap, but he was not bothered. He had heard worse. He broke ribs for a living. He didn't care that the man had dropped to the ground while he kicked the man's stomach violently. "Mr. Owen was nice enough to give you two extra weeks to pay your rent. Don't be ungrateful."

The man whimpered and sputtered curses stubbornly at Tarzan. His belly was already on fire and he had nothing else to lose. Tarzan kicked him again.

"Trust me I don't want to return to this place. I don't want to see you again and I suspect the feeling is mutual." The woman was bawling on the floor and her sounds were a little distracting for Tarzan. He almost felt unusually empathic towards her.

"Don't cry, lady," he said as he turned to the woman. "Just tell your husband to man up and pay his bills," and with those words, he left.

Tarzan and his partner considered themselves a collection agency which they made a lot of money from. They didn't mind that it required an immense amount of violence, as long as it was earning them money.

When Tarzan's partner hadn't shown up to work one morning, he became suspicious. In an attempt to investigate the reason behind his absence, Tarzan visited his home. He discovered that his partner had been shot. His body lay lifeless by his door and everyone walked over it. When an ambulance came to retrieve him, Tarzan realized that the shooting inferred a message. Whoever had shot his partner wanted him dead, too. He knew he had to leave. In a bid to escape, Tarzan then relocated to Miami.

At that time, cocaine wars were rampant in the state of Florida. There had been a transition between the Cocaine Cowboys and major traffickers like the Falcon Brothers, Sal Magluta and the Medellin Cartel. They were smuggling drugs worth billions of dollars from Columbia. Miami was the "drug capital of the world" due to the ensuing drug wars and uncontrolled bloodletting on the streets. Russians also flooded into Miami mainly because South America was so easily accessible. There was a wide variety of criminals from spies to drug dealers to murderers.

Tarzan blended in easily upon arrival. He was in love with the city. The air, the sand, the sun; they all called his name. He had found his home. He was ready to live and die in Miami. In 1991, Tarzan gathered his earnings in Miami and bought a strip club. He had acquired the club in the most unexpected way.

He had rented a shop in a building where he sold furniture. He collected fairly used furniture and sold them at exorbitant prices. While he was there, he was invited by the owner of his building to the grand opening of his new club. His name was Bill Siedle and also owned a car dealership that made waves in Miami. Tarzan refused to pass up such an opportunity. Such invites usually went with recommendations and new connections. Tarzan needed it. He dressed professionally and arrived at the club in time for mingling. While he socialized, police officers barged in and arrested the owner. While he was led out, the man stopped in front of Tarzan.

"This is yours now," he said.

"What is mine?"

"The club. If you want to run this place successfully, you have to be smart," he advised. "I will be locked up for a long time and I will hate to see my building go to waste. Take the club and pay me when you can." A policeman urged the man towards the entrance, and he moved.

Tarzan was smart when it came to his finances. He purchased the club as soon as he could. He had gathered his earnings from his previous job that included arson and debt collection and he was willing to pay almost immediately. Tarzan hated to be a borrower after having a lot of experience with debt collection. He had been ruthless to people and he didn't want to suffer the same fate.

The club barely needed to be cleaned up as it was almost running when he acquired it. He named it after his favorite movie, Porky's. One of Tarzans 'achievements was that the movie 'Porky's' was filmed in his club. He was so proud. After he had purchased the club, he ran it like a private one. In a few months, he realized that he needed a manager. Tony Galeota was recommended.

'Fat Tony 'Galeota was born on Long Island in the late sixties. When he turned sixteen, his father had got him a job as a wedding DJ. The gig introduced him to a crazy world.

Prostitutes attended weddings constantly, and they were very easy to spot. They would wear the most revealing dresses or try to look simply innocent while sneaking their phone numbers into the pockets of random men.

> "Call me," they would whisper and walk away suggestively. They were not bothered about the wives and girlfriends that attended the ceremonies with the men. They only came to do their jobs.

When he asked an older employee where they had come from, he was taken to West End, Manhattan's infamous strip club. The technique in which the women pole danced exotically while wearing almost nothing, enticed him. Not before long, he began to patronize them. He became a pimp who introduced his friends to strippers and got paid for each blowjob they received.

Galeota graduated to car robbery for the Paccione clan which was also tied to the Gambino family that Tarzan worked for. He stole various items from suits in strip clubs to electronics in secondhand car parking lots. With the money he gathered, he became a loan shark. Always willing to give, but brutal to people that didn't honor their payback dates. Galeota's father was ashamed of him, but when he lost his job, Galeota became the breadwinner.

By the age of eighteen, Galeota had been arrested seven times, but he was only given a few months of probation each time. In an attempt to lay low, The Paccione clan sent Tony to manage a club called Pompano Beach. He transformed the place in a short period of time. He also fell in love with a waitress named Kristy. It was easy to woo her. All he had to do was convert the club to a better version of itself. Kristy liked hard workers and she was attracted to his mysterious alter ego. She knew that they had very similar traits.

One night, there was a fatal shooting by one of the workers in the club. The electrician simply walked in after being fired and began to shoot people whom offended him. It was a very messy scene and he fled right on time. Two days later, the shooter turned himself in. After he was arrested, the club was forced to close down abruptly. Tony and Kristy found themselves jobless in no time. Tony was lucky to receive information from his friends about a Russian who'd just opened a club in Miami that needed an experienced helping hand.

When Tony Galeota arrived at Porky's, he transformed yet another club. where he introduced music and professional strippers to the place. One of the new features involved a stripper and a dildo. For as low as five dollars, she would lay on a table and allow a client to drive a dildo attached to a toy car into her vagina. Men always gathered around the table.

"Go faster!" they would yell to the man with the remote.

"Harder! Make her scream."

Occasionally, there were competitions for who did the best job. It was always the highlight of the evening and people loved it. In the first month, they had made sales of about fifteen-grand. Within a year, they were able to make one hundred fifteen-grand per month. By the mid nineties, Tony Galeota had turned the club into a perfect one-stop shop. One could acquire strippers, sex and drugs in one visit. Prostitution was so rampant that the club had to regulate the prices and locations for sex. It was simple; one hundred for a VIP room and one hundred and fifty or more for sex.

With the growing popularity of Porky's club, it became a home everyone; especially criminals. The club was the roughest in the area. It was common knowledge that the club was owned by a Russian and Porky's became their hangout. It was a place where one could easily be killed. Tarzan always carried two guns for protection. He had a Berretta attached to his hip and a Colt tucked in his ankle holster. Russians flooded the place from different parts of the country and Tarzan became the go-to person for both Americans and Russians in all of Southern Florida. He was resourceful and could get anything done; moving drugs, providing prostitutes and assassinating people. He made a lot of money doing this.

The law enforcement agencies feared that Russians would collaborate with the Columbian people, combining their drugs with the Russian military hardware and become a huge uncontrollable threat to South Florida. A task force was created to curb this, and was comprised of FBI agents, Marshall Service Drug Enforcement Agencies, US Customs, US Immigration, US Coast Guard and other local law enforcement agencies. It was called Operation Odessa.

CHAPTER 2

Tarzan's business allowed him to meet a lot of famous people such as basketball players and musicians. In the course of his dealings, he met Vanilla Ice, an American rapper, actor and TV host who was born in Texas and raised in South Florida. Around the time his music had begun to make waves, he met Tarzan.

"Could you help me take this boat out for repairs?" he inquired.

It was a 42 Tempest speedboat. Tarzan had no idea where to get a boat fixed.

"Where do you want me to take it?" he asked instead.

"I have a friend who owns Fort Apache Marina," Vanilla Ice told him. "He'll know what to do."

When Tarzan met Juan Almeida, he liked him instantly. The man was a tall, shrewd and intelligent businessman and Fort Apache showed proof of that. He was also a striking and charismatic man and good looking, too. The ladies loved him, and the men respected him. He specialized in hiding away assets for people before they went to jail and selling them off before they returned. He was so smart that he always found a way to get out of tight corners. He could take one's boat before the person was sentenced to jail, vend it and sell another boat to the person when he returned from doing time. Even then, they would still be acquaintances with no anger festering between them. He was amazing.

Fort Apache Marina was a playpen for the rich and famous with the likes of Julio Iglesias and Gloria Estefan as loyal customers. It was also a meet-up spot for drug dealers. They could easily pull their boats out and sail away after their dealings. Juan was known for selling boats, cars, motorcycles and anything on wheels to wealthy people. He had only one rule and that was he never wanted to know what the items he sold would be used for. He only preferred to do his part.

"Don't tell me what you need it for. I'm not a cop," he often said.

Juan was also known to have some dealings with the Cali Cartel. It was a drug cartel formed by the Rodriguez Orejuela brothers and Jose Santacruz which was based in Southern Columbia around the City of Cali. At the peak of their reign, they were said to control almost all of the world's cocaine market. They were also rumored to be responsible for the expansion of the cocaine market in Europe. They had connections with British mercenaries and Israelis among others. By the mid 1990's, the Cali Cartel had become a multibillion-dollar enterprise.

When the Mercedes SL 500 had just been released, the Cali Cartel called Juan and asked for half a dozen of them for Columbia.

"How soon can the cars arrive? The boss wants to give his men a treat for the holiday. He would like them to be decorated according to the Christmas holiday spirit. A little red here and there," the voice said.

Juan had not been opportune to meet the man in charge. Most of their conversations were done over the phone through an assistant.

"You can get them as soon as you'd like. Should we expect any financial misunderstanding?"

"No, Cali does not owe anyone."

They placed the order like they were buying mere donuts. Juan did not let the opportunity slip from his fingers. It was a good chance to forge a great relationship with such an influential group. He flew to Switzerland and ordered them from a Mercedes dealership. Afterwards, he loaded them onto a cargo plane and sent them to Columbia. They were glad to have the SL 500 before anyone else and it fueled Juan's reputation.

After Juan and Tarzan met briefly, they began to do business together. It was simple. Tarzan identified the buyers while Juan brought the suppliers. They shared the commission. On a daily basis, they would have conversations about moving the products back and forth.

"Someone wants to buy shrimp worth three thousand pounds and I told him that would give him about fifteen hundred kilos. Is that it?" asked Tarzan.

"More or less." Replied Juan.

"That is a lot of shrimp." Juan never wanted to risk the loss of any goods.

"Oh yeah?"

"It is definitely a whole lot."

"I thought so too. I wonder why they need that much."

"Well, don't worry about it. The more they sell the more we make.

On December 25, 1991, the Soviet Union collapsed. The hammer and sickle flag had been replaced by the Russian tricolor flag. Mikhail Gorbachev resigned as president of the Soviet Union after losing control of the soviet republics. Boris Yeltsin became the president of the newly independent Russia. This led to an increase in crime rates, drastic cultural changes and social upheaval. Corruption was at its peak within the Russian government. Law and order seemed lost in Russia. No one knew who was in charge. The collapse of the Soviet Union felt like a Christmas gift to Juan Almeida. Everything was for sale. He scored items at outrageously cheap rates. He could not believe his luck.

When Juan and Tarzan wanted to buy motorcycles at a factory about a hundred miles to the east of Moscow, Juan suggested that they should charter a helicopter to move the motorcycles. Tarzan was a bit skeptical as he expected the rates to be over the top. When he called the military air base, he was stunned.

"Good morning. My name is Tarzan," he greeted. Anticipating the worst.

"How may I help you?" a lady on the line asked him.

"I would like to rent a helicopter," Tarzan told the lady.

"Rent?" she asked in confusion. "We don't rent out helicopters." Tarzan was beginning to lose hope.

"But, do you have helicopters?"

She paused. "We do. There are about four hundred helicopters here. However, they have not been used for a while because we have not been able to maintain them or provide the required gas to fly them."

Tarzan was a little confused. "Four hundred? How much would it cost to rent one?"

The lady paused again. "May I call you back? We have to calculate the expenses we would have to make before we give you a final figure."

"Of course. Thank you," he said.

For the entire day, Tarzan waited nervously with Juan for their call. When they called back, he snatched the phone anxiously from the receiver.

"Hello?"

"Good evening. I am calling from the agency. You called earlier regarding details about chartering a helicopter."

"I did," Tarzan nodded. "Were you able to come up with a figure?"

The lady cleared her throat. "I'm sorry. You're most likely not going to rent it because it is very expensive."

"How much is it?"

"The MI 17 with three pilots back and forth will cost you $500."

Tarzan almost fell out of his chair. "How much?"

"Five hundred dollars," the lady repeated.

"I know that it is expensive, but I am ready to rent one," Tarzan said finding it difficult to hold back his laughter.

When Tarzan told Juan, he laughed so hard. "Let's get ten of them and fly into the place like we own it!"

Tarzan laughed and shook his head. "You drink too much."

The helicopter service in Moscow happened to be more impressive than Juan and Tarzan expected. When they arrived at the military air base with their rental fee, they were expecting that someone might try to bully them into paying extra money. They were stunned that the price remained the same. They only had to hand the money over, and the helicopter was theirs to do as they pleased.

The pair got on the helicopter right after the pilot that was appointed to them had approved. He greeted them courteously and obtained permission to take off. Once the helicopter was airborne, Tarzan breathed in a sigh of relief.

They had reached the center of the city when the pilot spoke.

"Where would you like to go?" he asked them.

Juan bent his head towards the pilot to avert the noise.

"Rachitic Motorcycle Factory in... Do you know the place?"

The pilot stayed silent briefly and Tarzan was beginning to assume that he knew where they were going based on the confidence that he oozed.

"I am very sorry, but I don't know where you're going," the pilot said in a rushed sentence. Only Tarzan heard.

"What did you say?"

The pilot shrugged. "I don't know, but we can just ask for directions. It's fine." Tarzan became irritated.

"This is a helicopter not a taxi."

"What are you talking about?"

"You will see."

True to his words, the pilot touched down near the curb of a major road. As he approached the ground, people ran back and forth to avoid the helicopter while others came out of their hiding places to see the helicopter up close. Most of them had never seen a helicopter before and they assumed we had come to earth from the moon. Tarzan could barely appose his lips to contain his shock while Juan's eyes were the size of saucers.

"Is this even allowed?" Juan asked, but the pilot ignored him.

Instead he alighted quickly without parking while Tarzan followed closely behind. A middle-aged woman with shopping bags stood at the curb while others ran. She didn't mind the harsh sounds coming from the helicopter or the strong wind that the blades had gathered. It almost seemed like she expected to see a helicopter in the city.

"Excuse me Madam. I'm trying to find Rachitic Motorcycle Factory In"

"I know that factory, son," the lady said. "You need to fly this way." She pointed a finger towards the right indicating more specific directions. Tarzan could not withhold his excitement. He loved the place.

The pilot followed the woman's directions strictly until they arrived at the factory. They were still buzzed when they landed in a parking lot nearby. As they alighted from the helicopter, they spotted a police officer and the euphoria died. He had a stick and a whistle. No sign of a gun anywhere, but they were still concerned that he might delay or completely obstruct their mission. They approached him cautiously.

"Good day officer," Tarzan said too loudly and brightly.

The man was not moved. He looked at them like they were aliens. "

Who are you?"

"We are from Moscow."

The countenance of the policeman slowly changed. His confidence disappeared and his shoulders fell. One could easily see the fear in his eyes.

"Oh...okay," he stammered. "What do you need me to do?"

Tarzan smiled. "I need you to stay and watch this helicopter." Obediently, he took a stance in front of the helicopter and wore a serious frown like one on a mission. It was almost humorous.

Juan and Tarzan went to the factory and they were provided a tour. There were thousands of motorcycles of various colors covering every inch of the ground. Tarzan sat on one of them as Juan made the business deals. He was in charge.

"How much will one of the motorcycles cost us?" he asked the owner.

"About two hundred and fifty," he said unsteadily. Juan was an impeccable businessman who was great at haggling. However, he knew that the bikes were worth more than he was getting.

"Look at how this will go. We will buy thousands of your motorcycles at two hundred for one," he said simply. "Do we have a deal?"

The man pretended to think about it. He knew he was about to make the best deal of his life.

"How many thousands are we talking about?"

"Two hundred and fifty."

"Thousand?" The man could have easily swooned.

He swayed slightly and supported himself with one of the motorcycles. He cleared his throat quickly and tried to sound professional again. "From what you have explained, you would like to purchase two hundred and fifty thousand motorcycles?"

"Precisely."

"How soon will I have my money?"

"As soon as I see my motorcycles and confirm that they are in great shape," Juan stated.

"We can start immediately!" the man said. He was doing a great job at hiding his excitement, but Tarzan could still sense it. He didn't blame the man for his reaction. He would probably do worse if he were in his place.

Juan and the owner of the factory signed a contract and almost immediately, they began to organize motorcycles that would be transported to the United States.

Before Juan returned to Miami, word had it around the entire country that there were bikes for sale. It was the talk of the town. Cartels were picking them up by the dozen for their security. Private security companies wanted Juan's new bikes. A few people wanted bikes just because everyone had one. The motorcycles were extremely easy to sell.

After all the expenses, Juan made a million dollars in sales. He rewarded Tarzan promptly for his services and they remained business partners.

CHAPTER 3

Nelson Tony Yester was the brain behind the Juan Almeida and Tarzan Fainberg. Tony Yester was an international fugitive long before he met any of them. Before he went into hiding in 1990, he was a secret service agent in Cuba and a pilot in Miami who transported drugs to different countries. He was a renowned international drug smuggler who spoke Spanish, English and German. He had passports for more countries than anyone could count. Even he was unable keep up with it. He travelled extensively and he knew how to disappear. The cops were always three steps behind him. The closest they've ever come to him was when they discovered he had a British passport under the name Hector Santana. He lived in South America for most of his criminal years, but he always moved around. He would travel to Cuba illegally and send a postcard to the US Marshall Office in Miami where he had been charged for drug trafficking. He loved to destabilize them despite the risk and his postcards always had the same pattern.

'Hey, I'm at the beach sipping a mojito and I don't see you guys here. When are you coming to pick me up, huh?'

It was an enjoyable exercise for him. Taunting the police was the best part of being a fugitive. There were other perks. He had connections all over the world from Amsterdam to South Africa, to Columbia and Venezuela. He had a *guy* for everything. Apart from that, Tony was one of the few people who worked directly with Pablo Escobar and had dealings with the Medellin Cartel. His reputation preceded him.

Tony Yester arrived in the United States in May of 1980. As soon as he arrived at Key West and the boat disembarked, he became overwhelmed. The place looked like paradise to him. There were so many people on the streets who were so elegantly dressed and pranced about as if they owned the place. The fleet of cars that moved on the roads were surreal to Tony. He knew it was the kind of life he wanted ultimately.

"I need to find an easier way to make money," he muttered to himself. He wanted to be able to afford the lifestyle he craved. He wanted a Ferrari. A Chevrolet was beginning to look like a joke to him. After debating with his inner self, Tony walked into a gun shop and bought himself a 357 magnum.

Tony Yester heard about Juan Almeida before they met. Juan was the king of the black market when it came to cars. He could get Ferraris from Italy before they were even announced and Lamborghinis long before they were released on the market. He was a great salesman, and everyone knew him in Miami.

When Tony wanted to buy his Ferrari, a friend of his directed him to Juan's warehouse, Fort Apache. Tony walked in and was impressed. It was a huge warehouse with countless sleek cars that came in various colors. After he had looked around and made a choice, he was directed to Juan's office to make a deal.

When Tony walked in, he got the warmest invite, and instead of letting him sit, Juan took him outside to show him around by himself. Unfortunately, the car that Tony wanted had already been sold. Instead of letting Tony go away empty-handed, Juan showed him more cars with even better features. After Tony had made his final decision, they walked back to Juan's office. The two men sat there for over four hours talking about everything and nothing. They knew immediately that they would become great friends and be great assets to each other. It was a match made in heaven.

After Tony left the warehouse, two men approached Fort Apache in a Lamborghini and asked to see Juan. They were both dressed in dark suits and tinted shades that shielded their eyes. They appeared very shady, but most of Juan's customers were just that. They were directed to his office and with a warm welcome. The customer service at Fort Apache was impeccable.

"Gentlemen, welcome to my place. How may I help you?"

The men were not fans of the introduction. Most of Juan's serious clients did not beat around the bush. They knew what they wanted down to the color of the foot mat. The poor hagglers usually found it difficult to decide.

"We are from Columbia. I heard great things about you, and we are here to purchase speed boats," the taller one said. "Can you get us some good ones?" he had an oddly shaped beard that would normally put Juan off, but he pretended not to notice.

The customers were always right and perfect in his eyes. Besides, they looked like they could make him much richer than he was.

Juan didn't want to ask what it would be used for. He could guess and the question had always been bad for business.

"Do you have any specifications?" he asked instead.

"Just two. Speed and distance. I need something that can navigate through international waters at the fastest speed possible."

"We can do that," Juan nodded.

"How fast do they go?"

Juan paused. "I have boats now. Beautiful boats that you would love, and I'm ready to give them to you. However, if you prefer a continuous supply of these boats, that may also be arranged to better suit your taste."

The other man sat up.

"Explain."

Juan smiled at his achievement. He had their attention. All he had to do was take hold of it like a lifeline.

"All I'm trying to say is that we could make custom engines and add turbines that would make the boats much faster than they are now. When we are done, the boats will be able to compete with planes in speed. Also, you will be our sole consumer. I presume you won't be happy to hear that your competitors use the same components."

"We will take the boats you have now while we await your custom made boats."

"It will cost you," Juan said.

"Send us the bill."

The first boats that Juan sold to them were cigarette speed boats which were stealthy and fast. They were difficult to detect except while in a calm sea or at close range. They were also difficult for security agencies to incept. They moved as fast as Juan had promised they would and are capable of traveling long distances. However, the custom-made boats were even better. They covered great lengths in a very short time and when they approach the shore, they sounded like planes. It wasn't uncommon for one to look up in search of the sound of the source upon its arrival. The men were happy, but Juan was happier. He made a couple of million dollars on each boat.

One day, when the men from Columbia had returned for another delivery, they found helicopter brochures from Moscow on Juan's desk. The helicopters were called Kamov KA32. That model was a high performance heavy-lift helicopter. They were so strong that they could pick up five thousand kilos on a hook and more than three tons inside. The men became curious and picked up one of the brochures.

"What is this?" one asked although the men already knew all about the helicopters and their capabilities.

Everyone in the drug business had heard of the KA32. It was a prized jewel. Juan had been scribbling away on his account book. He looked up to see what they were referring to. When he noticed the brochure, he shook his head.

"Those helicopters are not for sale. I'm trying to negotiate with someone to get turbines for them."

"Everything has a price," the man said simply. "We want specialized helicopters for our operations. We know you haven't disappointed us yet, but we want to know if you can handle this for us as well."

Juan didn't think for long. "Of course. I should be able to purchase them for a million dollars," he said easily. He knew he could get them at cheaper rates, but it was a business strategy.

"We can give you a million and five hundred if you can sell us two of these helicopters."

"Gentlemen, you have yourselves a deal," Juan replied as he boldly extended his hand.

He had been right about them. They were going to make him very rich.

The Cali Cartel heard about the business transaction early on. They wanted to ensure that nothing would get out of hand as a routine precaution. Tony Yester was their first port of call. Tony had just left a business meeting when he received the call.

"Hello?"

"My man, Tony. How are you doing?"

Tony recognized the voice. The Cali Cartel never called to discuss anyone's health or the weather. He knew they wanted something from him.

"I'm fine. I trust that you are fine too and business is excellent," Tony said.

"Business is always excellent Tony. What do you know about Juan Almeida?"

Tony and Juan had become friends since their first meeting, and he felt defensive.

"He's a good one."

"Of course he is. I just need you to keep an eye on him. He's been making some big moves and we want to make sure that it doesn't come in the way of our business. You know we can't lose a dollar on an American."

"He is not an American."

"He might as well be. Keep an eye on him."

"I will," Tony finally giving in.

In a few days, Juan was ready to purchase the helicopters for his new business deal. Tarzan had become his partner after the motorcycle deal, he wasn't left off of the new contract on the table. To fulfill his promise to the Cali Cartel, Tony Yester set a meeting with Juan at the Hilton in Caracas.

Tony was at the restaurant when Juan and Tarzan arrived. Juan approached him with more excitement than Tony had prepared for.

"Hey Tony, give me a hug!" awkwardly, Tony obliged. Juan was too nice to be rejected. After they had moved aside, Tony noticed the man behind him. He looked like a huge Russian bear, staring at him in admiration. It was almost creepy.

"Who is this?" Tony asked suspiciously. Tony had been running for too long to be caught easily in such a clumsy situation.

"This is Tarzan!" Juan exclaimed vigorously. "I've told you about him already."

Tarzan approached Tony in an admirable fashion. He stretched his hands out and Tony hugged him as well. Tarzan immediately liked the man. He looked very handsome and Juan had told him how smart Tony was. It was difficult to dislike him, and Tarzan wasn't even trying. It was also difficult to ignore that all the women were staring at him. Tarzan was slightly jealous of.

"What are we having for lunch?"

A waiter approached them, and they placed their orders. While they waited, Tony wanted to talk.

"So, tell me about yourself," he said to Tarzan.

Tarzan shrugged reluctantly.

"I'm a business man."

"We are all businessmen. Tell me something else,"Tony laughed throwing his head back.

"I own a strip club in South Florida. It's called Porky's. Just like the movie," said Tarzan.

"Not the Porky's story again," Juan said rolling his eyes.

Tony was confused. "Was the movie filmed in your club?" he asked.

Tarzan nodded vigorously.

"That must have been very good for business, eh?"

"Very good."

The waiter arrived with a bottle of wine and filled their glasses. When he left, Tony continued his interrogation again.

"How cute are your ladies? I might just visit you when I'm nearby. What do you say?" Tony asked.

"A friend of Juan's is a friend of mine. I will give you my best room and my best girls for free," retorted Tarzan.

Tony chuckled. "I like you. What else do you do?"

"A little business here and there. I do what Juan does." He turned to Juan. "Did you tell him about the story of the motorcycles?"

"Of course I did," Juan said as he turned to Tony. I told you about that crazy time that we landed in the middle of a street in Russia."

Tony cackled. "I remember that crazy lady with the shopping bags that said, 'fly this way 'to your pilot."

The three men exploded with laughter. Tony was great at imitating voices and oddly he sounded just like the woman although he had never met her.

"You ...you're good, Tony," Tarzan sputtered in-between giggles. "Tell us about you. You must have a thousand crazy stories."

Tony shook his head. "I like you too much to tell you anything about me that will potentially implicate you. My name is Tony Yester although I have forty-one other names. The United States has rejected me although I still visit and send the bloody cops a post card when I'm around. That's all you need to know for now. The stories will come later."

Tarzan was silent for a while. The awkward moment hung like a cloud over them.

"That's understandable," Tarzan said eventually. "We just met and I don't expect you to trust me. I'm sorry for crossing the line."

"No need to be. This has nothing to do with trust. Let me tell you something funny. When I saw you behind Juan, I thought you were a bear that had broken out of its cage."

Juan could not hold himself. He almost choked on his wine.

"Tony! You're insane! Why would you think that?"

"Don't you see how huge he is? I thought he was going to eat us all!" Tony said.

Tarzan started laughing. "I think you need to add some flesh to those bones. You look like you sacrificed all your muscle to the Atlantic to keep the police away. Did you?"

Tony held his midriff and bent over. He laughed so hard that his face became flushed.

"Touché! I like him, Juan."

"I told you he was the funniest," Juan returned as he slapped Tony's back.

The three men sat for three straight hours laughing at themselves and sharing their stories. It was difficult to make real friends in their illicit line of work, but they automatically trusted one another. It almost came naturally.

CHAPTER 4

Gregory Grisha Roizis sat quietly in his corner. He had never been quiet. In a different part of the world, he had once been considered untouchable, but Bulgarian prisons could bring out one's humble persona. It was simple. The prison guards assure you no matter how great you are in the real world, you'll be treated like trash in their kingdom. In the first few months, Grisha had tried to rebel against them, but they kicked and battered him so badly that he lost all his teeth. It didn't help when they heard of his old nickname: the cannibal.

> "So they call you the cannibal, eh? You eat human?" they used to tease him. "Don't you dare do anything stupid. We usually eat great food, but we're willing to downgrade to eat trash like you."

Grisha was lucky that they didn't know the real origin of the name. When he was asked, he cooked up a silly story.

> "Nothing really," he lied effortlessly. "A lot of people just thought I was strong then."

"Well, let's see what you've got," the guards had challenged him.

If it were a fair fight, Grisha might have been able to tackle one or two of them, but there were five of them. All of them held metal bars. After that day, Grisha could not walk upright for a full week. When he eventually recovered, he was given twice his usual duties to compensate for his absence the previous week.

If the police or even his fellow inmates knew the real reason behind the nickname that Grisha possessed, they would sentence him to an untimely death. Grisha was infamous for his violent ways. He could snap a person's neck without a second thought, and he was known to beat people to death. He was a major heroine dealer in New York, and he had been trying to expand his business at the time.

When he was arrested, he was in the middle of a major deal. Most would have tried to run or surrender upon realizing there was no chance of escape. Not Grisha. He was so upset that, as handcuffs were clasped to his wrist, he turned around and bit off the agent's nose. The man bled so badly, but it did not concern Grisha, nor did the name calling that followed. If anything, he liked the name; until he walked into the worst prison in the universe. There, he was merely a mouse among kings, and he wanted to remain invisible.

Grisha had been arrested in New York for major heroin trafficking schemes. After court ruled a sentence that was near life imprisonment. Somehow, he was lucky to make bail despite all the incriminating evidence. When he was released from jail, he left the United States. He was arrested in Bulgaria and charged with drug trafficking again. He never would've been in the hellhole he was in if he had stayed back. Maybe, he would've been respected in the United States jail. He had a reputation there. Outside the national borders, he was nothing.

Agent Philip was the first guest he had ever had. No one had bothered to check on him ever since he was roughly thrown into prison. When he saw the man, it was difficult to hide his joy. He was glad to see a different face.

"Gregory Grisha Roizis," the agent said.

Grisha had no teeth in his mouth at the time. Speaking was difficult, but he was able to talk to the agent.

"Yes, I am Roizis."

The agent did not waste time with small talk. He knew prisoners didn't like to hear it and he didn't want to instigate violence of any kind. The agent scratched his nose abruptly and pulled out a piece of paper.

"This is really simple. How badly do you want to leave here?" the agent asked.

"I'm ready to give anything. Even my life."

Grisha would normally be suspicious of the man. Police ever helped drug traffickers without putting their lives more at risk. However, in that case, he had no care if they cut out the pope's body parts piece by piece and sold them to the beef market. He just wanted to get out of prison as soon as he could. He had a brief vision of his room where he slept on the floor each night. He couldn't sleep on the cold hard floor anymore, especially when the guards had a habit of waking people up by smashing a rod against their backs. It was a miracle that he could still walk at all.

"Once you get out of here, we own you. The DEA will use you as they please."

"At thy feet I lie. I will do anything," he joked. It was a terrible joke, but Grisha was willing to do anything.

"We want Ludwig Fainberg. You might know him as Tarzan," Agent Philip said simply.

Grisha paused briefly. He knew Tarzan enough to feel bad about the decision he was about to make. It took him forty-three seconds to choose the remainder of his future. Tarzan would've probably done the same if their places were switched. He would understand that it was not personal. Decisions like that never were. Someone just needed what he could provide in return for what he wanted the most in his life, freedom.

"Just get me out please. I'm even willing to arrest him myself," Grisha swore.

It was not difficult to clean Grisha up. He was given a decent place to live, a chance to shower and a new set of teeth. The only person in the country that knew about his missing teeth was Agent Philips. There had been rumors about his arrest, but no one could clarify. He was just going to reappear in the underworld like he had never left.

Grisha was introduced to Special Agent Brent Eaton who was the agent in charge of the operation. Being there were several people on the team, only Agent Eaton's name stuck. There was something about his name that revived Grisha's appetite. When Agent Eaton asked to see him privately, he walked to the interrogation room with his head down and his arm still linked by cuffs. He sat down so humbly that if Agent Eaton didn't know the man, he might have considered him repentant. Of course, that was outright impossible. The man was simply a hustler, willing to do anything to survive.

"You should know that we cannot offer you any protection unless we have real evidence to work with. Until then, you have to save yourself," said the agent.

"I guess rats like me don't deserve any police protection. You should probably be protecting yourselves from me," he bragged.

"Really? How so?"

Grisha did not reply. He could not come up with a suitable reply.

Agent Eaton rose. It wasn't his first experience with a hardened criminal, nor was it his fourth. He knew how to deal with them. He ensures that he was staring right into Grisha's eyes.

"First, you're not one to make any threats or else you'll be thrown right back into jail."

Grisha shivered violently. He started having nightmares and even when one casually referred to the prison in Bulgaria as a joke, he couldn't control his reactions and had started taking a toll on him. He clearly had disorderly stress from all the oppression he had received.

"I apologize. It won't happen again," he said.

"Good. Now what do you know about Tarzan?"

"Oh Tarzan, he owns this strip club and a lot of shady business goes on there. That is all I know," Grisha said. "But I am willing to learn more if you let me out."

"Before we continue, what name do you prefer to be called Grisha or Gregory?" we can't call you one name while everyone else calls you another," Agent Eaton commented.

"Everyone calls me Grisha except Tarzan."

"I thought Tarzan was just a random person that owned a club with shady business."

Grisha retraced his steps. "We grew up in the same neighborhood. We have a cordial relationship," he murmured.

"So this should be easy for you." Agent Eaton handed a slip to Grisha with a pen holding it so tightly that it almost broke. It had been such a long time since he held onto a pen. He couldn't believe that he was a step away from breathing normal air without requiring handcuffs.

He took quick short breaths before he took a large gulp of air. Agent Eaton watched him closely. Prisoners usually had the most interesting tricks and he couldn't wait to see what Grisha had up his sleeve. He was willing to wait for Grisha to be done with his theatrics. He was their only hope of gaining any progress in the case, but Grisha didn't need to know that.

"You must be really desperate to get me on a case that is this sensitive," Grisha said smiling sadly.

It was saddening that he had to be a snitch to get his freedom back. It was a very necessary evil. In some worlds, it might even be considered as good.

"You must be really desperate to consider signing this. I know you detest the blue collar," Agent Eaton taunted him.

His face was so close that Grisha briefly considered biting his lip off. The thought of returning to Bulgaria was enough to return his sanity to him.

"I am desperate," Grisha said as he scribbled his signature on the slip.

He had agreed to work with the government to provide any information that they needed which he could access. He felt like he was dealing with the devil. He consoled himself with the thought of Tarzan going to prison. It was definitely going to hasten his return to his normal life; *if they did not kill him first*. A lot of people in the cocaine world hated snitches. He might kill him for cooperating with the government. It was a disgraceful thing and it was punishable by death.

Grisha stared at his signature one more time and handed the paper over to the agent. There were a few things that were worse than death and that prison was one of them.

Grisha hadn't rushed to Tarzan immediately. He went through Galeota to get his attention. It was Galeota that informed him of Tarzan's restaurant that was sinking in the mud.

"I know you've managed a bar before," Galeota had told him. "Can you manage this one?"

Grisha was surprised and almost suspicious to his kindness. He had not been given an easy hand in a long time, and his paranoia had eaten too deep.

"I can fix his restaurant for him, but I have no idea why you're being nice to me," he said

Galeota laughed. "Two reasons. Anyone from Brighton Beach is considered family around here."

"What is the second reason?"

"Tarzan is in debt from his restaurant and if you can get seventy thousand dollars to get it back on track, then you can manage the restaurant and remit the funds to Tarzan."

Grisha thought about it for a while until he realized that he had no say. Agent Eaton didn't want to give him the money. "I will get back to you," he promised.

When Grisha was able to reach Special Agent Eaton, he was shocked at his response.

"I will get you the money."

Grisha did not hear from him for a full week. When he did, the man was true to his word. He handed the money over to Grisha and promised to murder him if he ran away with it. Grisha grimaced at his tone.

The next night, he took the money straight to Galeota.

"I have everything here, but I want to see Tarzan myself."

Tarzan recognized him immediately.

"The Cannibal!"

Grisha laughed. "Tarzan, I see that you're doing very well with Porky's."

"I am. I wish Babushka could do the same. Galeota tells me that you have good news. You want to manage the restaurant for me."

"Yes."

"Do you have the money?"

"I do."

"Then we have a deal."

Their handshake was interrupted by a gunshot. Galeota, Grisha and Tarzan run out of Tarzan's office together. Grisha wanted to take cover while Galeota and Tarzan went out to trace the sound. Someone had been shot in front of Porky's. A car had driven past and left someone's brain splattered on the pavement. Tarzan and Galeota were getting used to the recurring gang violence in the neighborhood. However, body parts laid in front of the strip club was not going to attract clients.

Tarzan turned to his manager.

"Get someone to clean this up immediately!"

"I'm on it, boss."

In minutes, the walkway was as good as new and the night continued like nothing had happened. Grisha finally reappeared after they had returned, but no one had noticed his absence. He had decided to stay away from trouble as often as possible. He was still on thin ice and he could not get involved in a scandal at an early stage. He had a job to do.

CHAPTER 5

Agent Brent Eaton had sent a crew over. They waited in the truck until everyone had left the building. Grisha Roizis, the new manager of Babushka had told the janitors that a team would be coming at night for the renovations. They were told to stay at home for a night. Even Tarzan had been forced to leave after Grisha had promised to close the restaurant once the renovation team had left. He went home to his wife and daughter.

Once Grisha gave the go-ahead, four men marched in dressed in overalls whose faces were hidden behind black caps. There were so many wires that it was nauseating. Grisha Roizis thought he would feel guilty for attaining the highest level of snitching. He was championing the bugging of his friend's restaurant and hiding behind 'renovations.' He was supposed to feel awful, but he hadn't felt better in years. He could almost taste his freedom.

There were bugs everywhere. One at the bar, one under each table and one in front of Tarzan's office. Grisha couldn't access it in Tarzan's absence but the men weren't worried. They were able to put one of the best bugs near the keyhole since it covered a longer distance. Once they were done, one of the them placed a call to the men in their van.

"How good is the sound?"

"We need one near the entrance." The man moved the phone away from his ear and informed one of his teammates. "Done. How about now?"

"I think it's perfect."

The men disappeared as quickly as they had come. In the morning, Grisha had another idea. He wanted to buy a camera.

"I thought of putting an honor board where we can take pictures of our clients and pin them to the board. People like that stuff," he insisted as he laid out his suggestion to Tarzan.

"How do you know that, Gregory?"

"Ask around. All I need is one week. If you don't like it, we can always stop."

"Fine. Get a camera."

Grisha took out money from the safe for the camera and kept it to himself. Agent Eaton had already provided him with one. At first, it was difficult to convince people to take pictures. Everyone in South Florida was involved in one illegal business or another, and no one wanted his face in the wrong place. Grisha explained what the pictures were for and occasionally joined. The turn out became more encouraging. He would take so many pictures and pin them to the honor board. There were different captions; best dressed, funniest, best taste in wine, best taste in music, most beautiful. The list was endless. The board constantly attracted more people to the place and over time, the turnover grew.

Each weekend, Grisha met with Special Agent Eaton to run through all the pictures. He would put a name to each face and also match the voices. Eaton usually had to spend the entire day transcribing wire tapes and tagging photos. It was exhausting, and unfortunately it was not bringing them close to the end of the case. Grisha began to lose hope over time.

When Tarzan suddenly began to buy cars and wear expensive clothes, Eaton wanted to know about it.

"What changed? Why's he suddenly flaunting his money?"

They were in Grisha's small apartment for the weekend and they were going through new pictures. Eaton had noticed that Tarzan's attire had become showier.

Grisha shrugged and gulped down half a glass of water.

"Word on the street is that he and Juan Almeida were able to deliver these spectacular helicopters to clients in

Columbia. Since then, they've been living their best lives. Tarzan is busier these days with numerous international clients," Eaton said.

"We need to get our hands on his phone. It has to be bugged," Grisha said eagerly.

"Not 'we'. That's your job. I've been doing mine and I have yet to receive compliments."

Eaton rolled his eyes. "Do you want me to hug you or buy you a trophy? What difference does it make if we're not getting to the end of this case?"

Grisha grunted. "I'm sick and tired of this crap. I can't be tattling on a trusted friend and still be getting pushed around. It's annoying."

Eaton pushed the pictures aside and looked up at Grisha.

"You must really miss Bulgaria."

Grisha disappeared into the bathroom and returned after he had emptied his bladder and calmed down. When he returned, Eaton was smiling.

"What is it this time?" Grisha asked.

"Don't worry. I have the perfect plan," Eaton responded.

CHAPTER 6

Tony Yester woke up abruptly as if he arose from the dead. The room was still dark, and he didn't make a move towards the lamp switch. There was something about the darkness that calmed him. He looked at the small ray of light that peeked through the keyhole and felt like something was wrong. There wasn't a creepy noise in his house, nor could he sense an intruder. He just had an itch.

The day that Tony Yester learned to trust his gut was the day that he almost got arrested. Something told him not to show up for a certain deal he had invested so much money in. It was a very rash and stupid decision, but it was the only reason he wasn't in jail. He had watched the building from the top of another and he saw DEA agents surround the building like bees around honey and they raided the place; taking with them every single person that had attended. There were other scenarios where he disobeyed his guts because the ideas were ridiculous, and he was almost killed. In one situation, he had been shot and it would've been fatal if he hadn't been able to reach his private emergency doctor to fix him up.

That morning, he had a strange feeling that the end of the submarine deal was near. Nothing had happened. No one had been arrested or even suspected of any crime. He had just spoke to Juan and Tarzan the previous night and both men sounded fine. Still, he grew worried. He was tempted to tell his friends about his gut feeling, but he knew they would never believe him. It sounded so ridiculous that *he* almost didn't believe himself. How could someone even talk about a gut feeling when they could earn thirty-five thousand dollars?

Tony Yester stood and tripped over the fluffy slippers that lay almost indiscernibly by his bed. They always made him itch. Irritated, he put them back in order before walking towards the door. He considered the trip a sign. He had to act fast before they caught up with him. Worst case scenario was that he would get arrested alongside Tarzan and Juan, but he had no plan of letting that happen. There were bigger and better plans ahead.

In two hours, Tony Yester was on his way to Columbia. He had arranged a second meeting with the Cali Cartel without Tarzan or Juan's knowledge. He did not exactly like to keep them out of the loop, but he didn't feel very terrible about it or anything that involved money.

He presented his boarding pass to the staff at the desk and was allowed to pass through. The passport he had chosen bared the name Riez Handez. It was a new name and he hadn't gotten used to it yet.

"Mr. Handez?" the man called.

"Yes?"

"Have a safe flight," the man said

"Thank you," Tony retorted.

Naturally, Tony took his fake passport back and advanced toward the departure gate. There was a pregnant woman next to him trying to caution her children. Tony had a habit of helping strangers. One would think he had such a great personality, but he only wanted to blend in easily. Anyone looking at the woman would think that Tony was her husband. He offered to carry one of her boys and her extreme gratitude radiated through her smile.

"I can't thank you enough," she said and she handed the boy to him. "Johnny, you better behave. This nice man will hold your hand, ok?" The little boy nodded.

"I will do better," Tony offered. "I will carry you. I'm sure you're tired of walking."

Without much registration, the boy stretched out his arms to Tony and he carried him easily. He finally had an excuse to walk very close to the woman and no one ever bothered men with their wives and kids. They were picture perfect.

The flight was uneventful. Apart from the occasional babbles from children, nothing else happened. Once the plane touched down, Tony became excited. The rush he felt was inexplicable. He grabbed his carry-on bag, waved at the woman with the children and disappeared.

Normally, the Cali cartel and most other cartels picked their guests up from the airport as a sign of respect. However, Tony had insisted on grabbing lunch first. He claimed that he had become fond of a certain restaurant and he only wanted to get his favorite meal from there.

When Tony had reached the restaurant, he met the chef who had become his fiend over the years. The man had become old, but his food was still topnotch.

"Tony!"

"Sebastian!"

"I've missed you boy."

Tony laughed. "You say that to everyone," he reminded Sebastian.

"That's true, but you're special and you deserve the chef's special," the man said wholeheartedly.

"That is literally your motto. *Everyone is special and deserves the chef's special.*"

"Fine. You win. What are you having, Tony? We have some *arepas* to warm you up while you decide."

Tony nodded. "I will have that. Thank you, Sebastian."

"Always a pleasure. The chef's special will soon be ready, but you're free to choose something else."

"What are you serving today?"

Sebastian smiled proudly. "*Cazuela de Mariscos* served with plantains on the side. You'll be glad you waited."

Tony shook his head. "I'm tempted but I will definitely be late for my meeting. What do you have now?"

"We have *fritanga* and-"

"I will take that, please."

"Coming right up."

While Tony waited, he thought of the call he had received the previous night. Juan had talked to Tarzan and they thought it would be best to disappear with the money whenever the Cali Cartel paid. They were greedy by looking for a submarine in the first place.

"You were right," Tony had told Juan. "They are too greedy."

What Tony did not tell Juan was that the idea he had come up with the previous night had always been the sole plan. There was no way in hell that Tony was going to get Cali that submarine. He knew the kind of money they would make from such a deal and he might lose money in the long run. He didn't like it. Ultimately, he wanted the money for himself.

The platter of grilled meat and plantains finally arrived, and Tony received a glass of white wine on the house. As usual, the meal was more beautiful than the last. Sebastian never disappointed him.

When Tony was ready to leave, he called the contact he had been given. In mere seconds, a driver drove up to the entrance of the restaurant and Tony automatically knew that he was being watched since he arrived in Columbia. At least they had seen him eating. He didn't even take any calls. He checked his bag for all the photos he needed, and he held onto them.

A young man came around the car and opened the door for Tony. There was another young man in the back seat, but Tony was not upset. He knew it was the norm. He hadn't travelled with a weapon as he expected them to take it from him and never return it. It had happened so many times that Tony stopped bothering. As long as no one was shooting anyone, that's all that mattered.

When Tony walked into the warehouse, he was led to a room that was different from the one he was used to.

"Where are we going?" he asked politely. He knew the younger ones we're usually trigger happy and he didn't want to upset anyone and die in a senseless reckless death.

"You want to see the boss, no?"

"Of course I want to see the boss, but this is not the way to his office."

"No it's not. He is in the cash room. He counts his money on Tuesdays."

Tony nodded and followed the young man to a big room at the far end of the building. Tony had always been exhilarated by the smell of new money. He inhaled deeply. As soon as he walked in, the air was suffocating but Tony didn't mind. He would be glad to drown in such a room.

"Tony, my boy! Come in," Tony heard, and he turned.

There, the Cali king sat on a couch that could've been mistaken for a throne. Tony was in awe of the man. He managed ninety percent of the cocaine transactions in the United States and eighty percent in Europe. He made billions of dollars in profit every year. The man deserved to be worshipped.

Tony had never known his name or even his alias. No one did. Some people rumored that only Pablo Escobar was privy to such classified information. Tony was more worried about the man himself than the name he chose to call himself. He hoped that the man wouldn't be too bothered about losing a few million. It was a stupid assumption to make, but he went ahead anyway.

"I see you're counting your eggs," Tony joked.

The man chuckled. "Force of habit. Any good news for me?"

Tony nodded and dropped the pictures he had been holding. He scattered the pictures arranging them accordingly, from one boat by itself to the other being with the entire group.

"I'm the man in the black shirt," Tony said as he pointed at one of the pictures.

He remembered briefly how Tarzan had teased him incessantly until he was grinning. He silently wished he had looked more professional.

"I can see that," the man said to him. "You were obviously happy, Tony."

"I was, and I would be glad to make you a happy man too."

"I trust you."

"The men need the money as soon as possible. You know that this is not the type of deal that one leaves hanging for long. If the police catch the scent, they will come after us with all their dogs."

The man seemed to think for a full minute. "You're right, Tony. It's time to pay. Are we giving them everything at once?"

Tony shook his head. "Oh no. We can't trust them. They'll run with all the money and we can't take that risk. We will pay in increments of three at thirty percent."

The man stared into the air and mouthed words that Tony could not hear. He assumed that he was trying to make calculations. He finally gave up.

"What would that be?"

"Ten million dollars."

"That's fine," the man said as he turned to one of his boys. "José, give Tony ten blocks immediately."

For a second, Tony thought the man had ordered Jose to give him blocks of cocaine, but the notion was corrected as soon as the boy began to drop stacks and stacks of cash into a briefcase. The counting took the longest and each second drew Tony closer to losing his control of his bladder. The experience was surreal. He couldn't believe that he was about to acquire so much money for next to nothing. He was eager to get his hands on the pile of cash.

Once the young man was done, he shut the briefcase and handed it to his boss. The man in turn handed it over to Tony. Tony took the case with all the reverence it deserved.

"Go and get me my boat Tony," he said.

"You know I will."

Tony couldn't leave fast enough. He tried to be as calm as he could until he got out of the building. He boarded a taxi straight to the airport as he had initially planned. He was able to purchase a plain black bag and he emptied the contents of the briefcase into it. Tony wasn't going to carry a tracking device across different continents. He left the briefcase in the trash can in the bathroom. At least they would know that he was traveling. No one could figure out that he was headed to Amsterdam.

It was easy for Tony to find his friend's house. The house was in the suburbs and Tony had been there so many times. He never had a business deal with his friend, but the man knew he was involved in something shady. Tony didn't care what he thought. He only cared that he'd be available to help him hide out whenever he needed to.

He placed a quick call with a burner phone.

"John, it's Tony," he said with ease. "May I borrow your house for a little bit?" It wasn't the first time either.

"Hey Tony! When did you get here? I'm out right now, but I'll be back in an hour. Do you remember the security code?"

"You know I can't forget. I'll see you when you get here." John had used his birthday as the code.

Tony thought it was the dumbest idea ever, but he said nothing. It wasn't the right time to patronize him.

"Good. I will be back as soon as I can. Help yourself to anything in the refrigerator."

Tony let himself into the house and went straight to his friend's garage. There, he emptied the bag in into an old box and stared at it. It looked and smelled like ten million dollars. Tony could not believe his luck.

"Fuck! Ten fucking million!" He knew the garage was soundproof like every other part of the house.

He touched one of the bundles raising it to his nose. The scent almost made him to start touching himself. There was no greater turn on in the universe according to Tony.

Five minutes passed before Tony could snap out of his euphoria and hide the money properly. Before he left the garage, he took out a stack of ten thousand dollars. Tony took a shower in his friend's guest room and pulled out a new shirt from his small bag.

Tony stuffed the money in the microwave, sat on a stool by the counter and waited for his friend. John arrived in thirty minutes.

"Hey Tony!"

"John, how are you?"

"I feel fine."

Tony pointed towards the microwave. "Open it."

"What's in there?" he asked Tony.

"Just open it."

John walked like a robot to the microwave and opened it. The clean money threw him back for a second.

"Tony, how much is all of this?"

Tony smiled. "It's ten thousand dollars," he said easily making John gasp. "I need to borrow your house, but I want you to take your woman and travel for two weeks. Make yourself scarce and don't tell a soul that I'm here."

"Just like that? I've always wanted to visit Spain!"

"Just like that John. If everything goes well, then you will have ten thousand dollars when you return."

"Say no more."

John disappeared into his room. In fifteen minutes, he had returned with a suitcase full of clothes. He called his girlfriend and told her to pack for their surprise getaway.

"John what is the occasion?"

"An early birthday present. I wanted to surprise you."

"Oh my God! I love you so much!"

John took his money and left the house almost immediately. Once he was gone, Tony locked the doors and turned on the alarm. Afterwards, he disconnected the phones and looked around for cameras. When he was sure that the place was clean, he returned to the kitchen and he poured himself a glass of wine. Then, walked to the garage. He had to see the money again. He had nine million nine hundred and ninety thousand dollars, but it still felt like ten million.

"Thank you, Cartel de Cali!" he shouted.

CHAPTER 7

Tarzan wouldn't leave his office often. Unless he wanted to attend to his favorite clients, or if he needed a quick service from one of his girls. For a place like Porky's, it was almost inevitable to have a lot of favorites. The club was always packed with people from across the globe. It represented the diversity in the United States.

That evening, Rico had visited from Cuba. He was Tony's personal friend and any friend of Tony's was automatically trusted by Tarzan. It went both ways. When Tony called him concerning Rico's visit. He had left all the bookkeeping that he was crosschecking and wanted to welcome him.

"Rico!" he said once he met the man in front of the club. "Please come in. Welcome to Porky's our one-stop shop. We provide only the best service here."

Rico seemed uncomfortable with the crowd, and Tarzan was glad to send him up to one of the private rooms in the VIP section. It was a win-win situation. He would be satisfied and obliged to spend more money than people normally would.

They were lucky to find a room as the rooms on that floor were usually jam-packed as well. Tarzan was ready to throw people out, but he was glad that he didn't have to. He led Rico to the finest available room and ushered him to a chair. There was a small bar at the corner and a bartender waiting to attend to him.

"What would you like to drink, Rico? We have everything here except beer which we don't serve in this section. We know you deserve better."

Rico chuckled. "I'll take vodka."

The bartender brought a bottle and poured it into his glass. Rico nodded absently to the soft music that seeped into the room. He liked the serenity of the room.

"Can I smoke in here?"

"Of course," Tarzan replied. He wasn't ready to leave yet. "We have a lot of amazing girls too if you wish. The couch is a makeshift bed."

Tarzan pointed towards a lever under the couch that Rico could pull. He pulled it and the couch flattened automatically. Satisfied, Rico stretched out on the bed.

"Oh I *definitely* wish," Rico replied. He pulled out a cigarette and the bartender rushed to light it.

"Coming right up," said Tarzan as he left his room.

He knew the girl he was going to get for Rico. Candy was his best girl. She knew how to ride a man at any pace he desired and put on the best performances. She came highly recommended. Her reviews had been great, and Tarzan had had a taste himself. He could attest to her dexterity.

Tarzan walked down the stairs to find Galeota. He was trying to make peace among two angry thugs.

"Galeota!" Tarzan called from across the room.

"Boss," he answered before turning back to the men. "Don't do anything stupid or I will call the cops on your asses," he threatened before walking towards Tarzan.

"Yes, boss?"

"Get me Candy. I need her for a special client," Tarzan said to him.

"Yes, boss."

Tarzan returned to his office assuming that all would be well. He had only spent twenty minutes on his books, before he was called again. Annie walked into his office to inform him of the chaos in the VIP room. He had instructed her that he always wanted to know if anything out of the ordinary was going on in the VIP rooms. It was usually quite peaceful. Tarzan had been lucky to bring men who didn't beat up his girls or make a mess. His luck had finally run out.

When he walked to the VIP room, he found Rico holding his hand to his chest. He was guarding the dorsum with his other palm. His face was contorted, and Tarzan knew he was in pain. *What had happened?*

Tarzan looked upset. He did not want Tony's visitor to go back to Columbia with terrible news. He couldn't handle that.

> "What happened Candy? You know the client is always right," he reminded her softly.

What he really wanted to do was to beat her. She huffed and puffed like she owned the place.

> "Not this time. He used the back of my hand as an ashtray. See!" she cried.

Candy shoved her hand in front of Tarzan's face and truly, there was a ring there that smelled burnt.

> "Who did you report to?" Tarzan asked. "We have a policy here."

She grumbled. "I reported the beating I got to Tony and he did nothing. I decided to take care of this one myself."

Tarzan looked at Rico again and realized that the man had been swearing under his breath. Tarzan hated the displeasure on the man's face. It was not good for business.

"What exactly did you do?" Tarzan asked menacing. He was more upset than his face let on.

She shrugged. "I simply poked the back of his hand with a cigarette. I was even nice about it." she watched as Tarzan's face transformed from expressionless to a brewing storm.

"Please tell me that you didn't hurt my client, Candy," he growled.

"I swear it wasn't that pain-" She never completed her sentence.

Tarzan raised his hand subconsciously and slapped the words right out of her mouth. She was stunned for two seconds right before he slapped her other cheek.

"Our clients are always, ALWAYS right! Do you know who he is?" Candy guarded her cheek protectively and shook her head no. "He is Tony's friend. Tony Yester's friend. No one disrespects a friend of Yester's in my building. How could you even conjure such insanity?"

Candy began to step back as soon as she realized that Tarzan was a ticking bomb that was ready to detonate. His cheeks were deep pink, and all of his veins had popped out. He looked like a nuke with a timer waiting to implode. He turned to the client and apologized with the calmest tone he could muster.

"I am really sorry, Rico. We will get you a more civilized girl. Candy is not at her best today," he pleaded.

"No need. I lost my appetite already. I have an early flight to catch. The man stood and left the room.

Tarzan's gaze followed him eerily. Once he had reached the door, he turned around and smiled.

"Don't you worry. I'm telling Tony that you have the best service here. They are all very courteous."

"I appreciate the gesture. In case you return next time, drinks are on me."

Tarzan fixed a smile on his face that lasted only as long as he could see the man. Once he was sure that Rico had left, he turned back to Candy.

"I hope you cans see what you have done. He barely spent any money. He will probably close some business opportunities that I might've benefitted from. He'll tell everyone what a shitty club Porky's is and news travels fast."

"It can still be remedied," Candy begged. She knew she was in trouble.

"How? Will you chase after him for an apology blowjob?"

Tarzan grabbed a chair and flung it towards her. Candy ducked down, but not in time. The chair slammed her arm just before it smashed against the opposite wall. She knew she was fired anyway and the only way to get out alive was to *get out*. Spontaneously, she turned around and ran towards the stairs. Tarzan ran after her. He had a big body like that of a bear and as he ran, the entire club turned in his direction. There were murmurs everywhere, but Tarzan didn't care. He only wanted to get a hold of the girl. Galeota who was addressing the bartender, ran after Tarzan to curtail the situation.

When Tarzan caught up with Candy, he grabbed a handful of her hair and banged her forehead against the hood of a car in the parking lot. When he raised her head, you could see a dent there.

"I'm sorry. Please. I won't do it again," she pleaded.

Tarzan had stopped listening. All he wanted to do was teach her a real lesson.

CHAPTER 8

Someone had just been shot in the club over a stripper. Two Russians had asked for the same woman, but one was more aggressive and would not wait his turn. Before anyone could blink, they were throwing punches. One broke the other's jaw and he pulled out a gun. Tarzan didn't make it in time to stop him from pulling the trigger.

Tarzan ran to the scene and disarmed the man before he could shoot another person. Fat Tony Galeota was right behind him. Tarzan punched the man in the face before his men dragged him out. His jaw was hanging by a thread, but he looked much better than the man who was sprawled on the floor and had become as white as a ghost.

"Galeota, why are you just coming now?" Tarzan barked. "You should be handling situations like this!"

"I'm sorry boss," Galeota replied. "I was paying some of our girls off."

"I thought payment was at 4am. What's wrong with you?"

"Small glitch boss."

"Get this man some help."

Tony Galeota knew the routine. The club was a no-cop and he knew the bleeding man could not be traced back to the club. He called one of the bouncers.

"You know what to do, Steve."

"Make sure you don't dump him anywhere around here. The last one you left in front of our parking lot died and the police was questioning the boss. He didn't like that."

"It won't happen again."

"Good."

The man on the floor steered slightly, but he looked like he was losing consciousness. Steve jacked his limp body and walked out majestically. Almost immediately, someone appeared and wiped the blood off the ground. It only took a few minutes for the club to return to normal.

As Tarzan returned to his office, he found his assistant tucked behind her desk.

"Anna darling, you look beautiful today. You should be downstairs, strutting your beautiful hips."

Anna laughed. "I'm happy here."

"Doing a boring job? I'd love to see you dance. You look like you would be great at it."

"I am, but I prefer a desk job."

Tarzan shrugged. "Suit yourself darling. Did I get any calls?"

"Just Juan. He wanted to confirm that you two were still flying to Moscow tomorrow," she said easily.

Tarzan slapped his forehead loudly. "For the helicopters! How did I forget about that? Please call my wife and get her to pack me an overnight bag. We'll probably spend the night there."

"I will do that, sir. Anything else?"

"Yes love. Don't call me sir. I might get into your pants one day." Tarzan chuckled at his joke proudly before disappearing into his office.

It was not the normal large office that most bosses preferred. It had a huge comfortable spinning chair with a mahogany desk which Tarzan adorned with pictures of his wife and his beautiful daughter. There was a section with couches for meetings with the big guns, but it was slightly cramped. Tarzan glanced at it his office with the bare wall that had been coated with dark paint. He knew it needed an upgrade. He was making enough money to fix the place up. He picked up the phone on his desk and dropped onto his chair. He dialed Juan's number easily.

"Juan, my friend. How are you?"

"I'm good. How is your little girl?"

"She won't stop smiling. I still wander how I was able to bring such a beauty into the world."

Juan laughed. "I think the same thing every day. I don't deserve those saints." He paused briefly. "We are flying to Moscow in the morning. The lady from the military air base said we should come tomorrow. Did Anna tell you?"

"She did. I will see you tomorrow, Juan."

"Yes you will."

Tarzan Fainberg and Juan flew to Moscow in the morning to purchase the helicopters. It wasn't difficult to meet with the right authorities as they had already created a personal relationship through the previous rental service that was rendered to them. When they arrived at the front desk in the abandoned military air base, they met with the same lady they've been communicating with.

"Hello beautiful," Tarzan said.

"Good morning. How may I help you?" she asked politely. She had the same smile plastered on her face.

"We would like to purchase some helicopters. We've already talked on the phone."

She looked into the book that lay on the desk and ran through the lines with her finger. When she spotted a name, she paused and looked up.

"Mr. Fainberg?"

"At your service."

"Please wait here. You will be called in shortly."

While they sat on the bench outside, the two men discussed their businesses. Juan told Tarzan about the Ferraris he had just brought in from Italy. Juan had endless stories about Porky's. He told Juan about the fight that occurred the previous night.

"Can you imagine? Those two idiots came to my club to fight over a cheap whore. She wasn't even that pretty and she charged the minimum. What did they want from that woman that the others couldn't offer?"

Juan shrugged. "Sometimes it's like that. She might be great in bed and they want a re-run."

"She is not that great, Juan."

Juan turned to him. "How do you know?"

"How do I know? I test run all my girls before I release them to the world. There are some amazing girls at Porky's, but she is not one of them."

"Tarzan!"

"Remind me to hook you up with my best girl. Her ass alone will make you want to worship her."

The lady approached them and interrupted their conversation.

"Gentlemen, we are ready for you." She led them towards an office at the far end of the hall.

When she let them in, Tarzan stopped himself from whistling. The walls were painted with a monochrome color scheme. There were paintings hanging on the wall with a few pictured that reflected the war. The new Russian flag stood proudly on the desk. Behind it was a stout man with a frown across his face.

"Good day gentle man. Please have a seat."

Tarzan pulled out a seat first, but Juan was the first to sit. He was eager to close the deal.

"How may we help you?" he asked.

"We are here to purchase the helicopters. Your secretary mentioned that you were made aware."

"You are the men after my helicopters. Of course. They only cost a million dollars each."

Tarzan and Juan were already aware that the start price would be that high. They were prepared to crash it to the ground. Tarzan's role was to look shocked and pretend the price was ridiculous. The same helicopters cost about ten million dollars in the United States, but the man didn't need to know that.

"That is just overpriced," Tarzan said. "How many of those helicopters do you have?"

"We have about six hundred of those beasts. They are all in tip top shape. The price is reasonable if you ask me."

Juan sat forward. "I will take two off of your hands if I can get them for five hundred thousand dollars."

The man smiled. "I like two. You look like good Russians. Because of that, I will take eight hundred thousand."

"Six hundred."

"Six fifty is the best I can do."

Juan stood and extended his hand. "You have yourself a deal. Where can I sign?"

Tarzan and Juan rented a cargo plane in the same military air base for two hundred and fifty thousand dollars. The Antonov 124 was a military plane that was humongous and could accommodate the two helicopters alongside some spare parts for the aircrafts. It was perfect for the job. Tarzan was able to acquire spare parts from a factory nearby before they were ready to leave. Juan went ahead of Tarzan to Florida to deal with some paperwork.

When Tarzan was ready to leave, the ground was covered in ice and the runway had to be cleared before the plane could leave the airport. As the plane taxied along the runway, Tarzan spotted six jeeps parked across the road. From each car, half a dozen men dressed in black fur stepped out holding the biggest guns and blocking the path. They looked angry and merciless. Tarzan considered running the over briefly, but he knew that they could shoot down the plane with one shot therefore, he wouldn't make it. Defense would be a terrible idea with more bloodshed than necessary. Tarzan instructed the pilot to stop.

They gathered the plane and formed a tight ring around it. Each one had a machine gun pointed at the airplane. Some of them held nukes. The pilot opened the door while Tarzan disembarked from the plane. Tarzan took a few deep breaths and silently prayed that it wasn't his last day on earth. He garnered all the courage in him and stepped towards the men.

"Gentlemen, how may I help you?" he asked.

"We know you purchased some helicopters from here. News travels fast."

Tarzan turned towards the voice and found two huge men that reminded him of apes that were unleashed to the unsuspecting world. Their necks were adorned in blinding chains that were worth more than cars. They carried such an intimidating aura that Tarzan had to resist the urge to step back.

"I purchased those helicopters legitimately," Tarzan said defensively. He feared that he would soon lose his bogus confidence and his voice would be reduced to a whimper.

One of the men laughed. "Son, nothing is legitimate around here until it has passed through us. You need to pay your royals, or you'll lose your life and your helicopters. Which one will it be?"

"I won't give you any money," Tarzan said. With a gun pointing at his right-side jaw which he hadn't noticed. He was drenched with sweat although the weather was harsh. The whole place erupted. Everyone was shouting "We want money! We want money!" Tarzan knew he was doomed.

One of the bosses raised his hand and the place became silent instantly. He turned to Tarzan with the fakest smile Tarzan had ever seen. "You chose your fate. Finish him."

"Wait!" Tarzan called desperately. "I won't give you money but I can get you cocaine."

All the guns that were pointed towards Tarzan were lowered automatically. He saw that he had their attention and he milked it. Tarzan had no connections across international borders, but he needed to keep talking in order to stay alive. He had no cocaine at the time, and he knew that Juan would not be happy with the idea.

"Can you really get us cocaine?" the man asked.

"Of course I can! Do you know Pablo Escobar?"

Everyone knew Pablo Escobar. Tarzan had read about him in the newspaper, but the men before him didn't know that.

"Do you know Pablo Escobar?"

"*Do I Know Pablo Escobar?* Of course, I do! He's my partner."

"Can you call him right now?"

Tarzan nodded. "Hand me a phone and I will call him right now."

A man walked to one of the jeeps and returned with a phone. He handed the phone to one of the men who gave it to Tarzan. Tarzan took the phone with shaky hands which he tried to hide. For a second, he stared at the keypad and completely forgot Juan's cell number. As soon as he recovered, he punched the numbers forcefully.

"Hello, Pablo!" Tarzan said with a high-pitched voice. Juan knew instantly that something had gone wrong.

"Tarzan, is everything alright?"

"Pablo, you need to get to Russia as soon as possible. We have a little problem here and I need you to come tomorrow to fix it."

"What is going on?"

"If you don't come, Pablo, I am a dead man."

"Ok Tarzan," Juan said nervously.

The next morning, Juan Almeida caught the earliest flight to Moscow. He had no idea what he was going to face or what he would say to get them out unscathed. When he landed in Moscow, a Lamborghini Jeep picked him up at the arrival hall and he was driven out of the airport. Everyone thought he was Pablo Escobar. Juan was lucky that he looked like the man. The resemblance made it easier to convince the men that he was really Pablo.

There was no law in Moscow at the time and it was not abnormal to find men driving around with their guns hanging out of their windows. Juan tried not to stare at any of their faces for too long. The men looked like they could be triggered easily, and he didn't want his body to be found lying carelessly on a street in Moscow.

They arrived at an office building and Juan was led to a large conference room on the second floor. He walked into the room and found that it was packed. Everyone awaited his arrival. Upon the arrival of *Pablo Escobar,* Tarzan sat at the corner of the room looking like a deflated balloon. Juan almost didn't recognize him. There were a few men that sat next to Tarzan and they looked as miserable as he did. Juan assumed they were the crew from the plane. Tarzan rushed towards Juan and hugged him tightly.

"Pablo," he cried. Then his voice reduced to a whisper. "*Act tough. Be mean.*"

Fear flashed across Juan's face briefly, but he recovered at that instant. He knew what he had to do. He was not expected to talk a lot. Each word he uttered had to carry a lot of weight. He had watched a few deals go underway in Columbia and he knew how get them out. Tony Yester had schooled him, too. He knew Tony would thrive in a murky situation like the one he was stuck in. When Tarzan released Juan, he took a seat directly opposite of the boss at the other end of the table. Then he absorbed the man's gaze. He was ready for business.

"Pablo Escobar?"

"Yes."

"We don't want to make an enemy out of you. We are only here for business. We apologize for the unusual circumstance," the man said as he nodded towards Tarzan. "We did what we had to do." Juan remained silent.

"We knew that you purchased helicopters which you will need to ease the movement of your shipments. We only have one favor to ask."

Juan said nothing, but he urged the man to proceed. The man began to look more nervous by the second.

"First we need you to understand that we haven't kidnapped your men. They are more like guests than hostages. We've treated them very well and only want to partner with you. We want to be your reps here in Russia. We know everybody and we can move your product very quickly. We can handle your business easily," the man said with more confidence.

"I'm listening, what are your capabilities?" Juan asked in a deep voice.

He easily slipped into Pablo's shoes and he was playing the role impeccably.

"We will take about fifty kilos," the man said.

Juan glanced at Tarzan and saw that his partner's face reflected his shock. He could not believe that he had boarded a flight to discuss fifty kilos of cocaine. He could've easily moved two thousand five hundred kilos to five thousand kilos in the same trip. Their suggestion was almost embarrassing.

Juan leaned back on his seat and tapped his fingers impatiently on the table. All eyes were on him. Then he stopped and looked directly at the man across the table.

"You are really stupid for making a suggestion like that. Do you know how easy and wasteful it will be to move just fifty kilos? Did you bring me here to joke around?" Juan bellowed angrily.

Tarzan could not tell if he was still acting or if he'd become serious.

"The man stood abruptly and tried to assuage Juan. "We did not mean to insult you. Of course, we can do better than merely fifty kilos," sounding unsure.

"I will offer you a better deal," Juan announced. "Give me a safe house where I can be assured that my cocaine will not develop legs and disappear. Then, I will fix a few Columbians there, and it will be just like a tuck shop. You'd get what you paid for, easily. You don't need to purchase too much at a time."

The men in the room looked at each other and nodded.

"That sounds perfect. It's a good idea," they echoed.

"There is a catch. You need to move the products quickly. I can't promise that they will be around forever, and I need to see commitment from your end."

The man at the end of the table nodded repeatedly. “We will not disappoint you Pablo.”

“Then it is safe to say that we are now partners,” Juan said calmly.

The man at the end stood up suddenly and searched around.

“Tell the secretary to get us the best wine. We have a new partner.” He turned around and hugged Tarzan and took turns hugging everyone in the room.

The secretary entered the room almost immediately with a few bottles of tequila. Although Juan would have preferred not to drink, he knew that he had to show solidarity somehow. It was a small price to pay for the nightmare that they had just survived.

Juan delivered the helicopters in Cali, Columbia, without Tarzan. It was the most dramatic entrance that had ever been made. When the Antonov 132 arrived at the airstrip, Juan was standing with one of his, waiting to receive them. Juan couldn’t be more grateful for his presence. He had convinced the man to come along to the airport before the helicopters arrived. It had been a wise decision. The view was like watching the triumphal entry from the front lines. The plane moved along the airstrip until it came to a stop. Just as Juan expected, the nose gear opened up slowly revealing the first helicopter. Juan could see a smile forming on his client's face.

The helicopters were carted one after the other out of the cargo plane and the clients wanted an immediate tour. It was a short tour as it only consisted of the cockpit and the large cargo. The men continued to nod until Juan worried about their necks.

"You've done a great job, Juan," the man said proudly. "Everyone must know this." Juan needed the referral almost as much as he needed the balance which he was owed.

"I will appreciate that."

"I know what referrals can do for you as a business man. I will ensure that you have people lined up for your goods and services as soon as we leave. You've been a great supplier and you have kept your end of the bargain."

Juan knew he must have been overly impressed to utter more than a few sentences. The man usually didn't talk much.

"I hope that this isn't the end of business between us," Juan said.

He already knew that he had bought the man's loyalty. He was going to be a customer for life.

"Business between us will never end. I will always need cars and boats. My daughter's sixteenth is almost here and I will need a Ferrari for her and her best friend."

"They can be delivered as soon as you'd like."

Just as the man promised, Juan became the talk of Columbia. He had flown huge helicopters which could be used to move tons of cocaine from Moscow to Columbia. In a place like Columbia, it meant that he was a superhero. He could achieve anything he wanted. Not before long, Juan became a major car and boat supplier in Columbia. Most of the cartels' network wanted cars from him and no one else. Juan had a reputable customer service and he never failed to deliver.

Juan and Tarzan made more money than they had anticipated. The phone lines were ringing more often and there were always jobs on ground. Juan never failed to include Tarzan in his international jobs and Tarzan was a great partner.

CHAPTER 9

Tarzan drove to Fort Apache to meet with Juan. It was becoming their routine. Previously they often met for business discussions, but in recent times, they did everything together and they had no threshold for spending. Tarzan parked his car and went in to find Juan. He was rounding up with a client when Tarzan arrived.

"So how many yachts do you want?" Juan asked the old man.

The man looked like he had lived his best life and he was ready to retire with his own yacht. He looked at the yachts that were anchored to the Fort Apache harbor for the last time. There were ten, but Juan and Almeida had bought six extra yachts in their last trip. They were yet to arrive.

"I will take three. My wife will want one for herself and my son-in-law just got my daughter pregnant. He deserves a yacht, too," the man mumbled. "Three will be just fine."

"That will only cost you three hundred and ninety thousand dollars," Juan said.

"Pretty cheap, if you ask me."

"I told you, George. I always sell at affordable prices," Juan said.

To his greatest surprise, the man made a quick call and a middle-aged man walked in with a briefcase. He looked like the old man's driver. The briefcase which he handed over to his boss looked a bit frail and worn out. It looked like it contained a retired lawyer's old case files. Juan did not expect to see clean notes in it. The man casually took out a stack of ten thousand dollars and handed the briefcase over to Juan.

"This is your money, but I will need the briefcase back. It belonged to my father," the man said plainly.

Juan recovered quickly and called his assistant to take the case immediately. He was also led to the building to sign a few contracts and close the deal properly. Once the pair left with the man's driver, Juan scratched his bald head.

"That was a quick deal," Tarzan commented.

"I had no idea he was going to pay so quickly. I would have hiked up the price, but the man did not look rich at all," Juan complained.

"Do they ever?"

Juan looked at Tarzan's shiny shoes and shook his head.

"Of course they do. Your shoes are proof."

Tarzan waved it off. "Are we still going to Cancun for lunch? You said you wanted to eat Mexican food again."

"Definitely. I've been dreaming of that chef all day. She is so beautiful," Juan reminisced.

They had flown to the country last weekend after one of Juan's friends mentioned that they served the best meals. Juan wasn't sure if it was the chef or the cuisine, but he knew he had to return to that place to have a taste of both. Tarzan was more concerned about the food. Women in Miami were good enough for him. He had a club full of strippers already.

"Well, I've been dreaming of the *chef special.* I don't care if she has one eye. I just want to eat her food."

"And you will." Juan pulled out his cell and placed a call to his pilot.

The man was always on standby. Juan and Tarzan had developed a very expensive taste in the past month and most of their cravings required them to travel by air. It was either they had exotic meals or exotic women. Both always give them satisfaction.

When they arrived at the restaurant, they were glad to meet the chef and even happier that she remembered them. The duo would've been difficult to forget since Juan made a pass at the woman at every chance that he had, and Tarzan wanted to eat everything they served. It was Juan's turn to pay and Tarzan had no mercy while ordering.

"May I have taco chicken mole and chicken and beef fajita and also your radish slaw?"

The waiter nodded. "Of course." He turned to Juan. "Would you like anything sir?"

"Just get me a bottle of Chenin Blanc. Tarzan has already ordered for the two of us."

"No I haven't. Get your own food."

Juan looked like he might strangle Tarzan, but he scrolled through the menu.

"Just get me *chicken mole* Also, I would like you to tell the chef that I would like to see her."

"I'm sorry sir, but I thought she just left here a few minutes ago."

"Are you patronizing me? Are you trying to lose your job?"

"Of course not. I will relay your message to her."

"Good."

The men discussed the topics they knew best: business and women. Juan wanted to get more helicopters since the demand was hitting the roof. Tarzan had no problem with that. He was more concerned about the dancers in the club he had visited in St. Petersburg. He wanted a good old lap dance from any of them. Juan mentioned the yachts that were yet to arrive, while Tarzan decided to get one.

"I almost forgot. I need a yacht," Tarzan announced.

Juan was surprised "Why?"

"Why? I can afford one and I want to live the life that my family never had," Tarzan responded.

Juan rolled his eyes. "Of course. You just need an excuse to spend your money."

"I'm going to name it Porky's"

Juan laughed. "I think we have enough Porky's for an entire lifetime. Maybe you should name it after your favorite person."

“Definitely my little girl. Diana is a great name for a boat. It had to be in pink studded letters. Yellow is her favorite color, but I don’t want my yacht to look like a playground.”

“Pink is really girly, but we can make it work.”

“Maybe you can stud it on the house? We’re great friends. I deserve freebies too.”

“Oh shut up already Tarzan,” Juan joked as the wine arrived.

On their way home, Tarzan had called his daughter to confirm that she was on her way home. His wife had no driver’s license and lately his driver had been busy working with Grisha Roizis. They were renovating Babushka to attract more people to the restaurant. Tarzan thought it was a brilliant idea.

The phone rang twice before the housekeeper answered the call.

Fainberg residence. How may I help you?”

May, please get my cupcake on the phone.”

Tarzan did not have to wait long before his daughter’s melodious voice seeped in through the receiver.

"Hello papa," she said. She had insisted on calling him papa and Tarzan had never rejected the name. He was too much Ukrainian for 'daddy 'anyway.

"Hello cupcake. So, you are back from school?"

"I am, daddy," she replied gleefully.

Tarzan could imagine her jumping up and down as she usually did when she was allowed near a phone.

"When will you be back?"

Tarzan thought about the tight schedule and all the paperwork he had to do in Babushka before midnight.

"Soon baby. I hope you enjoyed your ride from school."

"In the limousine? I did. The seats are so shiny, but it's a little lonely in the back sometimes. Can I ride with my friends next time?"

"Of course, darling. Maybe you can drink orange juice in fancy cups as well. What do you say?"

Diana's squeal almost dislocated Tarzan's ear. He had to move the receiver away from his ear for a few seconds. When he returned, she was done.

"Thank you, papa. I love you."

"I love you too, darling. Don't ever forget that."

"Bye papa."

"Bye."

CHAPTER 10

The Cali Cartel was never late. Tony Yester had cleared his schedule, knowing that they would soon arrive. They had agreed to meet at one of his houses in Columbia. Tony thought it was a strange request since they always insisted that he came to them, but he obliged. He had no choice. They were his biggest connect and he needed their trust at all times.

Tony's phone rang loudly, startling him. The men had arrived. He sat comfortably in his armchair in his study as they walked in.

"Please sit down," he told them and pointed to the chairs that had been pre-arranged for them.

The men sat down slowly without saying a word to Tony. One was slouching more than the others with a pipe in his mouth. Tony smiled and faced him. He knew that he was looking at their boss. The man didn't come out often. He preferred to send people ahead of him. Tony suspected that the deal was going to be a big one.

"It is good to finally meet you. Drink?"

The man did not reply. Tony took the go-ahead and he reached for the bottle of tequila among others. He had heard the man was a huge fan and he didn't want to disappoint him. Deliberately, he poured the drink into four glasses and placed them on the center table. After taking a quick gulp of his, he eased up and became more comfortable.

"How can I help you?" Tony asked confidently.

"This is the deal. We want to get a submarine," the man said without a preamble.

He reached for his own glass and took a sip. The other two followed suit. They had been waiting for him to make the first move.

Tony Yester masked his surprise behind a smile.

"You can definitely get a submarine," he said easily. "But what exactly are you going to do with it?"

"Why do you ask?"

"If you are going to use it, then it must be a big job."

The man rubbed his jaw absently. "We want to use it to move product. Forty tons appropriately."

The poker face was gone, and Tony could no longer hide his shock. He sat up abruptly.

"Fuck! If I can get all of that blow, then I would have the biggest reserve of blow in the world!"

The man ignored his statement. "How much do you think it is going to cost us?"

Tony pulled out a pack of cigarettes from his pocket to buy time. He drew out a stick and lit it. Then he blew a cloud of smoke in the air. He thought absently about Juan's words. '*Every time you negotiate with these suckers, start high. You can come down but always go high.*'

He smiled at the memory and cleared his throat.

"I think that with fifty, we can get top notch equipment."

The pipe almost fell out of the man's mouth. "Fifty! Fifty what?"

"Fifty million."

"Are you not out of your mind?"

Tony had to think fast. "Yes, but are you looking at the numbers? You want to take fucking forty tons. Do you know how much forty tons costs? It's about a thousand dollars per unit and you get forty million dollars for the first trip. You've practically paid the whole thing."

After they haggled back and forth for a while, the man began to cave.

"Tony be straight with us. How much will this cost us?"

Tony leaned against his couch easily. "I think we can get it for thirty million and you can just pay five million dollars for the expenses."

"Can I trust you, Tony?" the man asked. "I want to know if I can."

Tony chuckled. "Of course not. I have a reputation to protect."

The man stood and extended his hand towards Tony. "Don't disappoint me," he said as he shook Tony's hand firmly. "People that do usually don't stay alive for long."

"Understood."

The man stood first and the others followed. Tony led them to the front door of his house. When they left, he was not surprised to see the convoy that awaited the man. The trio moved towards the Ferrari in the middle and got in. Tony stood with his hands clasped in front of him. He considered waving at them, but he knew that he would appear tacky and unprofessional. Instead, he stood there, humming away until they had all gone. Then he turned around and walked towards the door.

"A fucking submarine. These guys are crazy geniuses," he muttered to himself.

Tony's first move was to call Juan. They had a meeting in Mexico that day and he had a flight to catch, but he needed to share his thoughts first. He grabbed his phone and punched the numbers.

"Hey Tony! How have you been? It's been a minute."

"I've been good. I just scored the greatest deal in the universe."

"Tell me."

Tony paused as a strange idea occurred to him. "Why don't we meet in Mexico first? I don't want to say anything private on this phone in case it's tapped."

"Fine. Are we still meeting at three o'clock?" asked Juan.

He sounded a bit distracted and Tony could hear some voices in the background. He suspected that he was interrupting a business meeting at Fort Apache. Juan took his business seriously, but his friends were always first priority especially since they usually had business to discuss.

"Of course we are. You know I never come late."

"Nor do I. Tarzan is the late one."

"Whatever you say Juan."

The three men met at the Razi Ringer Hilton as they had previously planned, and they chose a table at the corner of the restaurant. Juan and Tarzan were thirty minutes late as usual, although they had come in Juan's private plane. The meal was meant for them to catch up, but because of the deal that Tony had brought, it became a business meeting.

"You're late," Tony informed them once they had reached the table.

He was already sipping wine from his glass as he looked at them in disapproval.

Juan ignored his statement. "What was the emergency?" he asked instead.

He didn't want to dive into the topic of Tarzan's inability to dress up in record time. He always took his sweet time like a woman on her wedding day.

Tarzan looked confused as he sat in his chair. "What emergency?"

A waiter approached the table to take their order and after he had left, they continued their discourse.

"What emergency?" Tarzan asked again.

Juan turned to Tony. "Tell us already. Are we in trouble?"

Tony smiled. "No. Never. Not while I am alive."

Juan took a sip of the wine that the waiter had poured earlier. He hadn't bothered to take note of his name, but he liked how it ran down his throat. He gave a satisfied sigh.

"Tony we don't have all day. How much are we making on this one?"

Tony laughed. "You're always trying to make money, Juan. Will you ever stop?"

Tarzan shook his head. "I doubt that."

Juan wore a serious face. "Of course I will. What do you all take me for? I'll stop as soon as Tony does."

Tarzan bent over and buried his hands in his face while laughing. "It's as good as never."

He knew that Tony could never stop dealing and making his millions. He loved the game almost as much as the mint that came with it. It was intoxicating and addictive.

He raised his hand until everyone stopped talking.

"Fine, I will tell you. I met these guys and they want me to get them a submarine."

As soon as the words left his mouth, the waiter returned with their order. Juan's mouth opened and as he stared in shock at Tony. The waiter ardently, displayed the dishes they had ordered, placing each dish in front of each person. Tarzan was less worried about the steak he had ordered although it was medium rare just as he liked it. It smelled heavenly, too, but his nostrils didn't usually work their best when money was involved.

"You can close your mouth now, Juan," Tony teased as soon as the waiter left the table.

Tarzan picked up his fork and dropped it. Then he jumped out of his chair.

"What do you mean? A Russian submarine?"

Tony laughed. "Keep your voice down Tarzan," he warned. "Yes, I need one of those big fucking beasts. I already told them I could get one."

"How much are they willing to pay for it?" asked Tarzan.

Tony gulped his wine before speaking. "Twenty million dollars."

He loved his friends, but business was business. Tarzan was still impressed, regardless. He whistled flawlessly like a Texan and nodded repeatedly. Juan looked less enthusiastic.

"How are we supposed to get a military submarine, Tony? Are you out of your mind?"

Tony shrugged. "I already said I could and they promised to kill me if I returned without it."

"They really said they would kill you?"

"Not in those words, but yes. We need to start looking."

Tarzan smiled broadly like he had just seen newlyweds.

"We will get you a submarine, Tony. We're on it. I know a guy who can get us what we want."

"Are you sure?"

"No. But hell if I don't try. It's good money."

When Tarzan returned to Porky's, he called Grisha Roizis. He wanted to know how his restaurant was going. He had leased it out when it was running at a loss and Grisha had not done a terrible job so far. The restaurant seemed to be attracting a few decent loyal customers and it was coming alive. Tarzan had not really expected Babushka to make any great returns, but he was happy that it was moving forward.

"Grisha, how are you?"

"Good so far. Are you coming around tonight?"

"Once I'm done with my girls, I will let Galeota handle all the good stuff and I will come over," Tarzan told him.

He was sitting on his desk and looking at some of the pictures Grisha had taken. He had told Tarzan that the pictures really livened the place. When he started taking random pictures of people and putting them on the wall in Babushka, Tarzan had seen what he meant. It brightened the place up. Tarzan ran his finger along the edge of one of the pictures and smiled at it. It was one with him holding onto one of the girls. The girl had taken off her bra in preparation for a private show for Tarzan and Grisha insisted on immortalizing that moment.

"Sure boss," Grisha said ending the call.

Tarzan called his friend Misha. He was one of those men that Tarzan had met in St. Petersburg. He was the general director of a factory that sold one of the spare parts he needed. They quickly became friends after Misha had helped him solve a lady issue. After finishing a business meeting, he had been horny and in need of a quickie to crush the urge in minutes. Misha had connected him to the best sex of his life. He had also informed him that he knew of all the ongoing sales from electronics to aircrafts and boats. Tarzan discerned that he had to keep his number.

Misha's phone rang three times before he finally picked.

"Hello?"

"Misha, this is Tarzan."

"Tarzan! It's been a while. How's that club of yours?"

"It's alright. I have a strange question to ask you."

"Go ahead. I'm listening."

"Is it possible to get a military submarine?"

Misha laughed. "That is crazy."

"I warned you."

"I will ask around and get back to you."

It only took two days for Misha to call back with news. Tarzan was almost reluctant to answer the call. He assumed that he would get a negative response. Misha didn't let him get a word out as soon as he answered the call.

"The answer, my friend, is yes. You can get it. The real question is this: do you want one with or without weapons?"

Tarzan laughed aloud and stood up. "Are you serious?"

"Of course. I got in touch with the admiral yesterday. He said that he got to the top and you can choose any model you want."

"Really?"

"You can even have more than one if you want."

"Really?!"

"Yes."

"Thank you Misha. This is really great news. This is the kind of news that I like to hear. I will definitely call you back."

Tarzan immediately called Juan. "Do you have good news for me, Tarzan?" Juan asked.

"Pack your bags, Juan. We're going to Russia."

"What do you mean?"

"I mean that we're able to get a submarine."

Tarzan ended the call and poked his own chest. He had to confirm that he hadn't died and gone to Russian heaven. He could not believe their luck.

CHAPTER 11

Juan, Tarzan and Tony arrived in Russia the following week. They had made plans to meet with the captain of the submarine in order to establish the terms of the deal and the cost of the submarine. They had been instructed to meet the men at a restaurant at the epicenter of the City of Moscow. When they arrived at the place, Tony drew back spontaneously. The captain had arrived with five naval officers and they had picked a long table right in the middle of the restaurant.

"There are so many of them," Juan whispered.

"Yes there are, but we're already here," Tarzan reminded him.

"I thought we were early."

"You know these guys, Juan. You can never be earlier than them."

Tony still could not move. "What if they want to ambush us? There's just too many stars at that table, I feel like I'm looking at the fucking sky."

Tarzan looked at the table. "What stars?" then he noticed the stars on their shoulders that denoted the rank of each of the officers. Misha had been right about one thing. These men were the top of the top. "Oh."

The captain spotted them and knew immediately that they were the men they had been waiting for.

"Fainberg?" he asked.

Tarzan stepped forward. "That's me. It is a pleasure to meet you..."

"Captain."

"It is a pleasure to meet you, captain."

"I came with a few admirals and they would like to hear from you."

Like three mice, Tony, Juan and Tarzan walked to the table with Tarzan leading the pack. Tony was almost expecting some American policemen to jump into the restaurant and grab him. The place reeked of non-civilians and it made him nauseous. The captain called the waiter to serve them drinks. When the waiter left, they commenced the meeting.

"So we hear that that you would like to purchase one of our submarines."

They nodded in unison.

"It's easy. We can get it for you if the price is right of course. How much are you offering?"

Tony cleared his throat and leaned forward. "We have seven million dollars for the deal."

The captain laughed. "That definitely won't work."

"How much, then?"

"Twenty."

"If you agree to twelve, then we have a deal."

"Fifteen," one of the admirals said. "That is the least we can offer."

Tony raised the glass in front of him. "You have yourself a deal," he said and they all raised their glasses subsequently.

Once the main agenda had been thrashed, the men proceeded to discuss trivial topics. They wanted to know about the United States and the President. They asked the strangest questions, but Tarzan always had an answer for them. Tony was glad to disappear into the background. Tony had zoned out briefly, before he found himself agreeing to something that he didn't understand.

"Tony, are you coming?" Tarzan asked. Juan didn't look like he liked the idea but tried not to focus on Tony.

"Of course. I'll go anywhere you ask me to."

In retrospect, Tony wanted to take his words back. The men wanted to go to the sauna to celebrate the deal that they had just discussed, and Tarzan was fully in support of it. When they had arrived at the sauna, Tarzan was the first to take of all his clothes. His big belly fell out like a big bowling ball. Tony looked at him in disgust as if he had no shame.

"Tony, take your clothes off. We can't keep them waiting."

"I'm not going in there. I'm not going anywhere with a bunch of naked, naval officers. That is sick, Tarzan," he complained. "How are you fine with this?"

Tarzan chuckled. "It's not that bad, Tony," he replied. "Let me tell you something about these Russians. You don't know anything about them."

"Educate me."

"It's part of Russian culture. If you want them to know you trust them, you have to go to the sauna with them."

"What does that mean?"

"It's just like saying, '*You've seen me the way I am. I have nothing to hide from you.*' So please do me a favor and take off your clothes as a sign of respect and vulnerability."

"Don't say that to me. I'm not a stripper."

"Just do it."

Tony looked flustered. He paced back and forth in the changing room. He finally stopped and turned to Tarzan.

"See man, I understand what you're saying, but I'm from Cuba. I've never even seen a sauna in Cuba. You can't expect me to take off my clothes here in Moscow with these strangers. I won't do it. No fucking way."

"Then the fucking deal will be off and it's all your fault!"

Tony sat on a bench in frustration and looked up to Tarzan.

"Just go in. I need to digest this a little bit. I will go in later."

Tony sat quietly on the bench and thought about the best way to take his clothes off without humiliating himself. He had always been a looker and he had a great body. It had less to do with an inferiority complex. He simply didn't like the idea of showing his body to a stranger. He kicked the air and tried to concentrate on anything except the door. It was difficult. The only images in his head had Tarzan and a bunch of fat old men laughing while soaking their naked bodies in water. It was repulsive.

The door bursted open and an excited Tarzan rushed in with a white towel tied around his waist. His protruding belly was distracting.

"Are you tired of playing?" Tony asked disdainfully.

"No," he replied. "You won't believe what is going on out there."

"What's happening? Are they trying to step up the price?"

Tarzan shook his head. "They're offering me nuclear weapons. Do you know anyone that needs nuclear weapons? Can we sell them?"

Tony jumped out of his chair. "Are you out of your mind? Keep yourself together. We're here for a submarine. That's it. We don't want bombs."

Tarzan looked deflated as he walked towards the door. Once he opened it, he turned around.

"Think about it," he said and shut the door.

Tony sat down and laughed at the absurdity of the situation. One minute they thought they were unable to get a submarine and the next, they were getting offers for nuclear weapons. Russians were unbelievable. Tony wanted to run away. He started pacing.

"These people are crazy," he shouted to the walls. "I could end up in an electric chair for this! What kind of crazy people am I involved with?"

Tarzan had to call Tony a couple of times before he wore him out. He looked squashed as he peeled his clothes off his body, piece by piece. At each point, he wanted to give up, but he eventually joined the men in the sauna. He had become one of them. He sat with them and pretended to enjoy their conversation. It took them hours to decide when they had had their fill. When they finally agreed to get out, it occurred to Tony that they could only finance the deal if they could get in the submarine.

"Why don't you ask them?" he urged Tarzan. "They seem to like you."

"I only got naked with them, Tony. It doesn't mean that we're now best friends."

"You know the submarine bases are tightly guarded. We can't have access to that facility if we don't get permission. We need to see what we are buying."

Tarzan stared down at Tony until he lost the staring contest. Tony was right. He was always right.

"Excuse me," Tarzan said to one of the Admirals as he dried his face and patted his body down. "Is it possible for us to see the submarine we are buying? We know its top notch, but we just want to see it."

The man shrugged as if Tarzan had asked for donuts. "No problem at all. Of course, you can see it."

The men took Tony, Juan and Tarzan to the submarine base. It was very easy to get past the security since they were walking with the shot callers.

Once they arrived in front of the submarine, the captain announced, "You're welcome."

Tarzan could not breathe and when he turned to Juan and Tony, he knew they felt the same way. Tarzan believed that they were in the secret naval base. It was overwhelming.

"I feel like James Bond," Tony whispered to Tarzan. "Like I'm in a 007 movie. How did we pull this off?"

Tarzan snickered. "I have no idea."

The captain walked them around the ship giving them a comprehensive tour. Suddenly they were masters in the facility. They knew where everything was, from the cockpit to the sick bay to the communications department. It was outstanding.

As they were stepping out, Tarzan felt someone forcing a strange object into his hand. He looked down and found a camera.

"Tarzan, just take a few pictures," Tony whispered.

"Pictures of what?"

"The submarine. What else?"

Tarzan tried to return the camera to Tony, but he wouldn't take it.

"Are you insane? They will have our heads."

"Then just ask them. They let us get on it in the first place."

"You know the answer, already."

Tony shrugged. “I don’t care how you do it. We need the pictures to convince those people that they are really buying a submarine. They won’t give us the money otherwise.”

Tarzan hated that Tony was right again. There was no easy way out of the situation. If he took pictures without permission, he was going to die. If he hadn’t, then they had wasted the trip. Their clients might think that they had downloaded pictures from the internet, and they were lying about the submarine. Tony had mentioned that they were crazy people. Like a puppet, Tarzan approached the captain and tapped him lightly.

“Excuse me. I have a stupid question to ask,” he said. They had just reached the pier.

The man looked puzzled. “Go ahead. What do you need?”

“Can I take a picture?”

The captain laughed. “You’re right. It’s a very stupid question. Of course, you can’t take pictures here. This is a military base.”

“We really need this,” Tarzan pleaded.

The man glanced at his desperate expression and scratched his head.

"How about two hundred dollars?"

Tarzan was appalled. "Two hundred dollars for a picture?" He assumed they only made two to thirty dollars in a month.

"Do you really need it, or have the terms changed?"

Reluctantly, Tarzan pulled out two hundred dollars from his pocket and handed it over to the captain.

"There you go."

The man took the money and smiled.

"Take all the pictures you want."

He took pictures of the submarine by itself. Then, he took separate pictures of Tony and Juan with it. He convinced the captain to join in while Tony took a picture of him and Tarzan with the submarine. It was almost comparable to shopping for a used car.

In order to celebrate, Tony and Tarzan went to a club in St Petersburg. Juan had declined because he was too tired to go anywhere after their tour. Misha had hooked them up again. When they arrived at the place, it was just like they had expected. The place was clouded with smoke from pipes in every corner. One could get high simply by sitting there long enough. It was beautiful. The women were glorious. Their bodies moved to the music like they had a degree in pole dancing. They knew how to turn a man on just by staring and their lap dances were indisputable, the best across nations.

Tarzan sat and stared while Tony latched onto a stripper he had met. At first glance, he was offering her money. After a few lap dances, he was professing love to her.

"I have found the love of my life," he told Tarzan excitedly.

"Tony, you are married."

"Nobody asked you, killjoy."

At some point, Tony disappeared. When he returned, he had a gift bag in his hand. He handed it to the lady and smiled.

"It is really expensive, but I think you are worth more," he drooled. She took it from his hand and smiled seductively. "Thank you, love."

"Wait, Tony is that not-"

"Shut up, Tarzan."

"How much did buy-"

"Stop talking." Obediently, Tarzan did.

It was almost two AM when they decided to leave. Tarzan stayed back to take care of the bill while Tony stepped out. While he waited for one of the waiters, Tony's woman slithered towards him and worked her hand up his right thigh. Tarzan's eyes almost left their sockets.

"I don't like your friend. I like you. Just call me when you can, and you will get it all for free."

She slipped a small piece of paper in his hand and pecked his cheek.

"I can teach you all the tricks I know," she whispered before she stood.

Once she walked away from the table, the waiter arrived, and Tarzan paid the bill. He was in a trance until he stepped outside and met Tony.

"What took you so long?"

"I'm sorry man, but your lady slipped her number in my hand. She said she likes me. I'm really sorry."

Tony was quiet for a second. Then he turned to Tarzan.

"You owe me that perfume."

"How?"

"I'm dead serious."

And he was.

CHAPTER 12

Special Agent Brent Eaton entered the empty conference room and chose the seat closest to the door. He knew he would have to move to a different seat or worse, stand for the entire meeting. There was a floral flower vase at the center of the table that contained fresh flowers. He had wanted the flowers removed a long time ago, since it was a good location for a recording device. However, he found that the scent that emanated from it very refreshing and often calmed his nerves.

Eaton tried to concentrate on the flowers as he awaited the arrival of the other members of the team. The extra time was an opportunity to run through the progress and the roadblocks they had faced in the case. They had managed to gather hours of wiretaps from the devices they had installed in Babushka. Unfortunately, the records, if presented in court alone would be walked upon by a mediocre lawyer. They needed solid evidence like a confession or a video recording. Neither Roizis nor Babushka would give him that. Their best bet was an insider in Porky's where Tarzan spent more time.

It took Agent Eaton a long time to find the perfect match for his new idea, but he did. Special Agent Alex Yasevich had worked with the Drug Enforcement Agency in New York for years as an undercover agent. The most beautiful part of the plan was that he had lived in Brighton Beach while Tarzan was there, and they might have known each other. Agent Yasevish knew the right way to communicate with Tarzan and win him over. It was not going to be easy, but it was going to work. Agent Eaton would make sure of it.

It was a minute to the third hour, before anyone started marching in. The US marshal greeted Agent Eaton before taking a seat. The other attendees entered in pairs and took their seats without looking up. Agent Eaton wondered if anything could possibly be more important than the case they had before them. The Russians were trying to collaborate with South America. Drugs meet guns. It was the most dangerous combination in the universe, and he expected everyone to be focused on a case like Odessa. It was five minutes past three when Eaton started the meeting.

"May I have your attention please?"

The room silenced and everyone turned to him. He wondered if they had even known he was there in the first place. Their faces had been glued to their phones since they arrived like teenagers chasing after hot dates. He found it very irritating.

"Good evening. Thank you for being here today," he continued.

Someone's phone buzzed loudly on the table and he grabbed it. He murmured a half-hearted apology and clicked away on the keypad. Eaton was now bordering on anger. He had always been easily distracted. It was one of his weakness. He knew he couldn't go ahead until the man was done with his text.

He is probably texting his ugly wife to cook him dinner, Agent Eaton thought angrily. He had not seen his wife since she announced that she wanted a divorce and he could finally propose to his work if he wanted. She had flung her ring at him and it caught his nose. The next morning, he had to lie to everyone that asked about his nose saying that he bumped it against the wall. He was so sleepy that he didn't see it.

"May I go ahead?"

"Please."

"Thank you. This meeting as we all know is about Operation Odessa," he started again.

The words had already been scribbled on the white board, long before everyone else had arrived. Underneath, there were pictures of Tarzan Fainberg, Juan Almeida and Tony Yester. There was also a picture of Grisha Roizis stuck beside Tarzan's photo. The picture of Tony Yester was blurred as it was taken from a strange angle. It looked nothing like Tony, but they had to manage. It was the last picture they took. Agent Eaton glanced at the boards briefly before returning his attention to the small group. He had stuck the pictures there himself.

> "A few new faces have joined us today. Detective Beabody and Detective Asand," he said as he pointed towards them.

They were sitting side by side and slightly away from the crowd. It was obvious that there were the rookies on the team.

> "They were assigned to this team yesterday from the CIA and they have been briefed on the happenings in the case."

Everyone nodded towards them before turning backing to Agent Eaton. He did not miss the impatience that was becoming obvious on their faces.

> "It is obvious that for a while, we have collected a lot of wire taps from Tarzan Fainberg's restaurant called Babushka. Most of the evidence is incriminating, but none will hold water in court. These men are untouchable. For this reason, I decided that we will need a new character; someone who can also deal in cocaine, but who can actually be trusted. Grisha Roizis has been doing a great job so far, but we need to do better. We need a video tape."

US Marshal Langdon scratched his beard. "Are we talking about introducing an undercover agent? Is it really necessary?"

Agent Eaton could not believe his ears. Why is no one else seeing the gravity of the situation at hand?

"Yes sir," he replied disapprovingly. He couldn't hide his disgust and he did not try do so. "It is really necessary."

"Do we have anyone on ground?"

It was one of the rookies. Agent Eaton didn't bother to acknowledge which one it was.

"Yes we do. His name is Agent Yasevich. He grew up in the same neighborhood as Tarzan. He should be able to gain his trust and gather all the evidence we need to sink these men," Agent Eaton explained.

"What if he is not able to? What is our plan B?" the US Marshal asked? He was beginning to infuriate Eaton.

"There is no plan B. Agent Yasevich has been trained well in this aspect. He had been an undercover DEA agent in the drug world for a long time. He has been transferred from New York and will be here by tomorrow."

After the meeting, everyone filed out and Agent Eaton stayed back. The Odessa case had been eating him for years. Miami had become an uncontrollable crime zone and he wanted to take the city back.

When Agent Yasevich met Grisha Roizis, Agent Eaton had expected a brief moment of awkwardness. Instead, they hit it off immediately.

"I know you from Brighton!" Grisha exclaimed.

"Yes. You used to live a few blocks away from me. Tarzan lived on the other side of the road," the agent said.

He had the Russian accent that Grisha and Tarzan shared. Agent Eaton could not be prouder of his choice. Alex was going to slide right into Tarzan's world without much effort. They already knew each other.

Grisha looked a little worried. "What if he knows that you are now a cop? How will that play out?"

Alex looked down at his frayed jeans and oversized shirt. "Do I look like a cop to you?" Grisha shook his head.

"Exactly. No one else knows except a few people and now you. I hope it stays that way."

Agent Eaton glanced at Grisha with an intimidating look. Grisha caught the threat and nodded in agreement. If he finished the mission alive and free, he might just come back to break Agent Eaton's skull. It would be fun for him.

It took a few days to get Alex Yasevich settled in a suitable apartment near Porky's. It was small and functional. There were no personal touches anywhere. Alex was used to living in such homes. He had been working undercover for a very long time. He could barely settle down and have a family. He was always on the move, but he liked the rush that it gave him.

When Grisha was ready to introduce him to Tarzan, he called an hour ahead of time. Alex took a quick shower and met Grisha at the street corner.

"Are you ready?"

"Born ready."

It was past midnight, the best time to catch Tarzan at Porky's. Grisha and Alex walked to Porky's and met Tarzan at the parking lot. Tarzan was forcing gravel down a woman's throat. She only had panties on, and her breasts were dancing around like oranges in bags. She was taller than Tarzan, but she was no more than twenty-two.

"Eat it, you bitch! Eat the fucking gravel!"

Grisha rushed to the scene. He had never cringed at a violent scene, but he didn't like that Alex was seeing this side of Tarzan. No one liked to be seen as a woman beater although they all did it.

"Hey Tarzan!"

Tarzan let the woman go and she dropped like a sack of balls on the ground. A red circle was visible on her forehead despite the terrible lighting. She was crying her eyes out and choking at the same time. Alex did not look bothered at all. He had watched people shoot themselves, eat their own body parts and cut people. The scene before him was like a children's cartoon.

"Gregory, how are you?"

"I'm alright. Let the lady go. Come on," Grisha pleaded.

"She slapped a client. Something about him slapping her butt too hard," he explained.

"Oh that is really bad for business."

"I know. I thought women liked that kind of stuff," Alex said.

Tarzan shook his head. “I’m not worried about what they like. I want my clients to want to come back. He was a real spender.”

“He will,” Grisha assured him. “I just brought a friend to meet you. He insisted that he wanted to see you again.”

Tarzan extended his hand to Alex. “You already know my name.”

Alex nodded and smiled. He had heard about Porky's and he had secretly wanted to meet Tarzan again to know how he was doing. It was unfortunate that fate had chosen such a controversial circumstance to bring them together. The face looked slightly familiar.

“I am Alex Yasevich. It is a real honor to meet you again Tarzan. I’ve always wanted to.”

“Oh please. I’m just plain old Tarzan. There is nothing else except I drive a few nice cars. A Ferrari here and a Lamborghini there. Nothing else."

The men laughed. Then Grisha slapped Tarzan’s arm.

“Tarzan, don’t you remember Alex?”

“Should I?”

"Of course! He used to live in Brighton Beach with all of us. He bought that shiny new bike that was the talk of the town that time."

"That red ugly thing?"

The men burst out laughing. They all headed towards Porky's together.

"I loved that bike," Alex said in his defense. "It could take me anywhere."

"Is that how you got to Miami?" Tarzan teased.

"You win. It was not that great. It only lasted for three months and I couldn't get a refund."

"What?!"

"The man I bought it from, fled as soon as I paid him. I should've expected it when he agreed to the first price that I offered him. It was too easy."

Tarzan patted his back. "I'm sure you are wiser now."

"Definitely. It is one of the reasons I came to speak to you. I heard you are the best advisor and middleman in all of South Florida. You know everyone."

Tarzan shrugged. "I can only try."

The men entered the club and found a table at the corner. Tarzan ordered vodka for the table and turned to Alex.

"I will be back as soon as I can. I only need to ensure that my guest is duly apologized to. Then I need to fire a certain employee of mine."

Grisha nodded. "Do what you have to do. We'll be here waiting for you."

The bottle was almost empty when Tarzan returned. Alex was still nursing his first glass, but Grisha loved his alcohol. Alex did not complain as long as his threshold was very high. Grisha was still surprisingly stable. Apart from a few slurs here and there, his communication skills were still top notch.

"I've taken care of the little problem and now you can have me all to yourself for the night."

"I am straight, Tarzan."

Tarzan chuckled. "I guess you can have one of my girls in the house. It is the least I can do for my family from Little Odessa."

"I would appreciate that."

Alex knew the rules. You were not allowed to reject gifts. They were always meant to be taken, whether they came as guns or alcohol or women.

To them, the word no didn't exist when involving gifts. You always had to take what they offered. Also, Alex had gone cold turkey for months and he was ready to break his fast.

"Good, man. Now, I'm listening."

"Well... I've been in the heroin business for a while and it had been going well so far. Now I hear cocaine is the new gold around here. I would like to get my hands dirty."

"And you need my advice?"

"I wouldn't be here if I didn't. I will also appreciate a few calls. I am trustworthy and I will owe you a big one."

Tarzan smiled. He liked favors. They always came in handy.

"That's fine. Any friend of Gregory's is a friend of mine too, Brighton Beach or not. I will do my best."

"Thank you so much."

"Tell Gregory to give you my number. You can call me in three days. I should have what you need by then."

"I will not forget this, Tarzan."

Tarzan smiled and slapped his back fondly. "I don't expect you to."

CHAPTER 13

It was Tarzan's idea to meet and Alex Yasevich chose to meet at a hotel. He told them there was construction being done on his home as an excuse and he needed to be safe. The real reason was that Alex was afraid that Tarzan might get suspicious and recruit one of his neighbors to follow him up. Also, he wanted to have an excuse for the non-personal vibe that the room gave off with no family pictures or personal touch of any kind. Most importantly, he wanted to be able to disclaim the camera he had set up if Tarzan ever asked.

The camera was in form of a radio which Alex had bought last minute at a spyware store downtown. He figured that the tape he was using would not be sufficient. They needed evidence that was so glaring that it was undeniable.

Alex placed the radio on the desk in the room. The angle was perfect as it showed the full face of the person on the opposite end. Alex could have easily kept his pseudo radio on the side, but he needed to protect himself. If anyone ever got a hold of the video and recognized him, news would travel fast, and he would never be able to work or walk around as an undercover cop again. He'd never be able to walk again, period. The people in the underworld were ruthless and unforgiving.

While Alex waited for Tarzan, he made a cup of tea to calm himself down. He was more nervous than he had anticipated. Tarzan was not exactly the friendliest person on earth and he always carried two guns to remind people he didn't take betrayal lightly. If he ever had the idea of Alex wearing a badge, he would be dead.

Alex sipped his tea slowly, until the last drop. Just as he stood to carry his mug away, he heard a knock. Hurriedly, he dropped his mug on top of the fridge and opened the door. He knew it had to be Tarzan.

"Alex my friend. How are you?" Tarzan asked. He shook off imaginary dust from his boots and walked in. Alex followed him closely.

"I am very fine. I thought you wouldn't show," Alex said. "I assumed you would be too busy for an old Brighton boy like me."

Tarzan chuckled. "I'm never too busy for anyone from Brighton. That used to be my home and it granted me access to this beautiful country. Anyone from Brighton is as good as blood."

"I am glad about that. Thank you."

Tarzan sat on a chair. It was only after Alex had sat on the wrong chair that he realized his mistake. He began to sweat profusely under his jacket. He had no way of convincing Tarzan to move. The colt that was peeking out of Tarzan's ankle holster reminded him of his looming death. He tried anyway.

"Tarzan, why don't you sit in this chair?" Alex asked as he stood up.

"This chair is fine. Thank you," Tarzan said easily.

He thought Alex was trying to crack one of his silly jokes again. Alex had a great sense of humor. Most Brighton boys, after all the hustle in that city, were known to lose all their humor.

"No, you should sit in this chair. I assure you that it is for the best," Alex insisted.

Tony's forehead wrinkled in a frown. He was becoming confused and Alex refused to back down.

"But I want to sit in this one. Is anything wrong with that?"

Alex cleared his throat. "Fine, I will tell you why you have to move."

"You won't like it," Alex said helplessly. "Remember that whore you gave me the last time?"

"Candy. What happened to her?"

"She sucked me so hard that I came all over that chair. It still smells of my spunk," Alex said and shrugged.

It worked. Tarzan sprang off the chair like there were thorns on it.

"You should have told me, man!" He dragged Alex out of his own chair. Then he turned to look at the back of his pants. He had to make sure that it wasn't wet.

"I tried to warn you but you wouldn't listen."

"I didn't need to know that."

"Sorry. What can I offer you?"

Tarzan looked nauseated. "I just lost my appetite, but I will take a beer," he said.

His voice had become unrecognizable. Alex could not help but laugh at his genius lie. He didn't care that Tarzan would probably think he was laughing at him.

"Quit laughing, Alex. That is really childish," he called.

Alex returned to the table with two beers. "I'm really sorry. I just can't help myself."

The two were silent for a while as they took the first gulp of their beers. Alex eventually spoke.

"So were you able to reach your friends?"

Tarzan nodded. "I was. Since you're new to the business, I thought I would introduce you to nicer people. You can meet the big dogs when you've had enough practice in the kids' field."

Alex looked offended. "What does that mean?"

Tarzan raised his right arm in apology. "No offense. I respect heroine movers, but heroine is not cocaine. The cocaine market is highly competitive with extremely cold-hearted people. I wouldn't like you to start on such rocky ground. I care about you," Tarzan explained.

Alex nodded. "It's fine. So, who are these 'nice 'people?"

Tarzan checked his jacket pocket for a piece of paper that he had stuffed in it before leaving his home. He pulled it out and unfolded it on the table. There was a list of names and phone numbers. They looked like aliases, but Alex knew that Special Agent Eaton would devour the list like a cannibal. The man could never stand the idea of cocaine dealing. Alex, on the other hand was irresolute. He had tried cocaine a few times and he had come to realize what all the hype was about. It was heaven on earth and although he swore never to do it again, he didn't like to belittle people's addictions.

"Look at the list and sleep on it. I would recommend that you go with Alejandro first before you get involved with others. He's more flexible with pay days. The others are not as nice," Tarzan advised him.

Alex nodded fervently. He looked at the paper one last time and folded it.

"Thank you."

"Stop thanking me. Life has been good to me. I am glad to share it with everyone else," Tarzan told Alex easily.

Alex nodded. "Life has really been good to you," he said as he pointed at the jacket Tarzan was wearing. "That is a very clean jacket. While you searched for that list, I wanted to beg you to stop manhandling it and ruffling it recklessly. It looks like it might have a soul."

Tarzan laughed. "At the crazy price that I bought it for, I suspect it might have a soul and a real heart. My daughter just said that she thought it looked nice on me and I had to get it. It helped that I could afford it!" he joked.

Alex laughed. “It definitely did. How do you make so much money? Should I open a strip club, too? Is there a ‘get rich fast’ class that I don’t know about?”

Tarzan almost choked on his beer. “You are crazy Alex!” he said. “Also, you’re not missing any classes. The money I get from Porky's is great, but it’s not that great. I just have an amazing friend that I do business with. We make a lot of money off of our deals.”

“What kind of deals are we talking about?”

Tarzan had always loved bragging about his business and the money he made. The man lived in the limelight.

“Simple. We sell anything from motorcycles to cars, and helicopters.”

“Helicopters?”

“Oh, yes. Military helicopters.”

“Sweet Lord!” Alex said reverentially. “We’re talking millions of dollars here!”

Tarzan smiled easily. “Yes we are. I’ll tell you a little secret.”

“Tell me, please. My bladder is about to burst. Can’t you hook me up?”

Tarzan laughed. “You move too quickly, but I will tell you our next big deal. A cartel wants us to give them submarines to move their cocaine across international waters.”

Alex's mouth dropped open. For a second, he forgot he had been working with a script in his head. His legs felt like jelly.

"They want you to provide them with a submarine?"

“That’s impossible, Tarzan. I’ve never even seen one,” Alex told him.

“Nor have I, but I know a guy and he might be able to get us a military submarine.”

“Military! It definitely can’t be from the US.”

“Of course not. It’s in Russia. Everything is on the black market now since the Soviet Union collapsed. Russia is the best place to buy anything. You will be surprised how much a car costs there,” Tarzan narrated.

Alex shook his head in amazement while Tarzan took the last gulp of this beer and froze midair.

"What is that?" he asked. His tone had changed too briskly, and Alex's heart started beating very fast.

"What?"

Tarzan was pointing at the radio. Alex followed his finger to his greatest nightmare. The radio still looked like a radio, but he knew that that wasn't Tarzan's question.

"I'm talking about that."

"What? The radio? It's been here ever since I got here. Does it look like your dad's?"

"Don't bullshit me, Alex. That is a camera."

Alex's heart flew to his throat and it was beating faster.

"Camera?"

"Yes Alex. Why is there a camera in this room?"

Alex turned to look at the camera. "How the fuck is it a camera? Is it shaped like one?"

He began to raise his voice. He hoped his anger might be able to deflect Tarzan's attention.

"It looks just like a camera I have seen."

Tarzan was right. He had visited the same spy store where Alex had bought the camera. He had bought one with Juan. They were recording a client that they had suspicions about. The 'radio 'in front of him also had the same color as the one they had purchased.

"You know what? Go ahead and tear it apart, but I hope you have a little change from your stash to refund the hotel management. I can't be bothered."

Tarzan stared at the radio for the longest time and gave up. He had never liked paying for damages in public places no matter how little it would cost him.

"Fine. It is not a camera. It really looks like one though."

"Whatever." Slowly, Alex's heart descended to his chest. "I was literally going to offer you a gift for all the information you have given me."

"What gift?"

"I know that with all your dealings, you would need to make a lot of calls abroad. I was going to offer you a phone that allows you to call people outside the country at no cost. Some computer guru hacked the phone and bypassed the charges."

Tarzan was impressed. The radio was long forgotten.

"You *were*?"

Alex managed a laugh. He had not fully recovered from the scare. All the while, he could not wipe the image of Tarzan's bullets in his skull.

"I was. I still am."

"Where is it?"

"I've not even seen mine yet. The boy said he would deliver them by the weekend."

"Is it possible to get more than one?"

"How many are we talking about?" Alex asked. "I might be able to cajole him. You deserve it."

"I just need three. I have friends too and I know they will appreciate this."

Alex nodded. "I will get them to you as soon as I can."

"Thank you. I have to go now. I need to pick up my daughter from school," Tarzan said as he stood.

"You have a little girl?"

"She is the cutest thing you've ever seen."

Alex walked to the road with Tarzan where he hopped into his Mercedes Benz. Once Tarzan had gotten in and buckled his seatbelt, he waved at Alex and drove off.

A few blocks away, Special Agent Brent Eaton was waiting on Alex to meet him with good news. He had sat in his car for an hour and fourteen minutes devouring donuts while waiting for the report. When he noticed Alex approaching his car, he wiped off the sugar on his hand and moved the box of donuts to the backseat. Alex got to the car and let himself in.

"Any news?"

Alex handed the radio over to Eaton. "He knew it was a camera."

"What?!"

"We got lucky. I managed to distract him long enough to get his mind off it."

"Jesus."

The men were silent for a short while. Eaton dropped the radio in his backseat and turned back to Alex.

"Did he at least say anything that was worth your while?"

Alex smiled. "It's all in there."

"Just tell me please. I can't wait that long."

"They're planning to purchase a Russian military submarine," Alex said greedily.

"A submarine?"

"You heard me."

"Sweet Lord!"

"Exactly what I said."

Agent Eaton and his team had acted very fast. Before the day ran out, he had provided Alex Yasevich with three phones. Alex knew that they were running out of time and it was important to get the phones across to Tarzan as soon as possible.

That evening, he visited Porky's again. He had considered wrapping the phones in gift wrap, but he eventually settled for brown envelopes. They could multitask for official and casual use.

After ordering a beer and paying for a lap dance, he was able to get Galeota's attention. The man usually went around the tables to ensure that his clients were satisfied. It was a good way to make people return and Alex respected that.

"How are you enjoying our club?"

Alex smiled. "Your girls are scintillating and their skills are out of this world."

"I'm glad that you're enjoying yourself."

Alex caught his arm before he moved along. "Do you need anything else?" he asked pleasantly. He looked like one who could end a life in a second. Alex had to be careful.

"Not really. I just promised to get some things across to Tarzan today and I was hoping to see him."

The man nodded. "What is your name?"

"Just tell him that it is Yasevich from Brighton Beach."

Galeota instructed one of the girls to inform Tarzan's secretary. While Alex waited to meet Tarzan, he ordered another bottle. He knew that people who weren't drinking, smoking or talking to girls in a club often appeared suspicious. Bouncers had been trained to recognize them and to throw them out. While Alex gulped his drink, Tarzan arrived.

"Alex my man! Don't tell me you already called these people. I told you to sleep on that list first," he said.

"I'm going to sleep on it. I don't want to rush into something so important."

Tarzan slid into the seat beside him. "Did you come to enjoy my girls or good music?

"None, although they are both pleasurable. My friend showed up with those phones. Apparently, he had extras that he was willing to sell," Alex explained. "I bought them for you."

Alex unceremoniously handed the envelope over to Tarzan. He opened it and pulled out one of the phones. Alex silently whispered a prayer of thanks. The envelope was a good choice.

"Wow!" Tarzan was in awe. "So, international calls are free?"

"I told you." They were not exactly free. The DEA would be paying the bill, but Tarzan didn't need to know that.

"Thank you Alex. I really owe you for this one."

"You already paid."

Tarzan chuckled. "With a few names? Oh please, let me thank you properly."

"Don't worry about it," Alex insisted.

"Take any drink you want on the house, at least. Please."

"I thought you would never ask."

The two men laughed. A few minutes passed before Tarzan returned to his office with his new phones. He called Juan immediately and told him the good news. They would be able to make thousands of international calls at no cost. He also called Tony, but he had no idea when next he would come to Miami. Tony moved like the wind. One could only see him when he wanted the person to.

CHAPTER 14

Juan heard the craziest stories in Fort Apache. Last week, someone wanted to buy a Lamborghini jeep for a woman he hated, just to spite her. This week, it was a man who was attending a wedding where he would meet his ex-wife and her new filthy rich husband. He wanted to rent the latest Mercedes Benz just to impress her. He was broke, but he insisted. He would not be mocked. Juan was not the type to let business go no matter how pitiful the story was. His job was to sell or rent out exotic cars. His clients only had to keep their problems to themselves. That part proved the impossible.

"Do you think she'll like it?"

"Of course."

"Do you think she will come back to me after seeing it?"

Juan pretended to think about the question. He knew the truth was a bitter pill to swallow, but he needed to find the best way to sugarcoat it.

"Maybe you should consider buying the car. That way, if she wants to go on a date afterwards, she'll still see the car."

Juan knew that no sensible woman would return to him if he was renting a car to impress her. Maybe she would agree to a quickie or even a long-term affair, but that was it.

The man grunted distastefully. "I can't afford one. Isn't it obvious?"

"Then a rental will definitely do the trick." Juan wanted the man on his way and the conversation was wearing him out. As he walked back to his office, his personal assistant stopped him.

"You got a call sir," the young man said.

"Who was it? My wife? Tell her I will be home for dinner tonight."

Peter shook his head. "It wasn't your wife. The person promised to call back in a few minutes. I thought you might want to be around to take it."

On cue, the phone rang, and Juan picked the phone.

"Fort Apache. How may I help you?" Juan recited.

"I'm trying to reach Juan, please."

"You're talking to him."

The tone changed from a professional tone to a more familiar one.

"Hey, Juan, how are you?"

Juan was confused. He didn't recognize the voice. "I'm fine..." The uncertainty was practically dripping from his voice.

"Of course you don't know me. I am the Cali Cartel. It belongs to me."

"Oh wow. It is an honor to speak to you."

"Thank you. I will be in America today and I was hoping we could go out together and get to know each other," the man on the other end said breezily.

"I will definitely cancel my plans to make myself available."

"I expect you to take me to the best club in Florida."

When the call ended, Juan turned to his assistant. "Please call my wife and tell her I'm not coming home for dinner with the kids. Make sure I sound very remorseful. Tell her that this place is flooded with clients and I can barely see past my nose."

"I already called her while you were on the phone. She thinks you're coming home for dinner."

"Then call her back. Fix it."

Cali as he often referred to himself, was the best company. He picked Juan up from the Forte and let him direct them to the best club he knew. There was a crazy club on the outskirts of South Florida where they had the best music and the most amazing women. Juan felt terrible about sending them anywhere else except Porky's, but he didn't know how the man would like the crowd over there. Height Club was less crowded and more cashy than Porky's could ever dream of. It was the right choice.

The man had come with a few of his disciples and the group drank more than they had in a long time. By midnight, they were all tipsy, but by two AM, they were all gone. They spent like people that were allergic to saving and the women flocked to them. It was a memorable night.

The men eventually left the club and were driven to their various lodges. Juan went home to his wife who wasn't exactly happy. Not only did hi miss dinner with his family, he had also come home drunk. It was not the first time.

She stood upright from the couch as soon as the front door slammed. She moved from groggy to upset in seconds.

"Juan, where have you been?"

Juan smiled. "Nowhere. I told you to stop waiting up for me."

"I am your wife, Juan. It is part of the job"

"I'm sorry. It was important," he drooled as he staggered to the stairs.

"Is that all I am getting?"

"Yes."

Juan looked at the clock near the staircase. It was a strange place to keep a clock, but his wife Susan thought it was cute. He let her do whatever she wanted with the house. As he stared hard at the clock, he realized that all the characters were dancing freely. But it looked like the sixth hour had just passed.

Juan woke up just before noon. His breath chased him to the bathroom, and he brushed his teeth to remove the foul odor. Once he was done, he took a quick shower. His head was still heavy, and he had a terrible hangover, but he knew he had to go to work. A glance at his phone satisfied his curiosity. A million and one people had called, and he had a library of voicemails to listen to.

The first was his wife's. She wanted to know when he would wake. She had made her magic hangover potion and it was in the flask. Also, she had left him breakfast in the microwave. He remembered a quick flash of his words earlier that morning. He could have been nicer to her.

The potion worked instantly. Juan couldn't name what was in the tea, but he was glad that he had drank it. He grabbed his keys and left for Fort Apache.

It was four in the evening when Cali called again. Juan was in the middle of a business transaction. He excused himself and took the call.

"Hey, Juan."

"Cali, I hope you slept well."

"Like a baby. Those beautiful women raided my dreams. In fact, I'm just waking up."

Juan laughed. "You definitely slept well. I'm glad we were able to go out."

"Me too. Can we meet for a late lunch?"

Only Cali showed up to the restaurant. The other men were outside, watching the car. When Juan arrived, he spotted the man immediately. His aura had a way of attracting people.

"Juan."

"Cali."

"How do I say this...?"

Juan paused. He didn't like the new solemn tone that the man had taken up.

"I hear that you know Tony Yester. He's your friend, no?"

"He is my friend."

"Unfortunately, I can't find Tony anymore. He has disappeared."

Juan showed genuine concern and confusion. "Did he tell you where he was going?"

"He promised to get me my submarine. He must have discussed that with you."

Juan chose to ignore the statement.

"I need you to show me where he lives," he said simply.

Juan knew that there was nothing simple in his statement. People like Cali did not ask for favors. They only gave orders and expected people to obey. Juan was not the one to defy men in high places. He had a business and a family to consider. His life was also very important.

"I can do that," Juan said as he struggled to cover his fear.

It was a difficult task. Cali led Juan to his car and ordered him to get in. Without much thought, he did. In the car were men who would have looked normal, but with the big guns they held so freely, they did not. There were two cars behind them which probably carried similar men with replica guns. Juan pretended like they were more or less for his protection. He didn't bother to confirm.

Under Juan's instructions, the convoy drove to a small homey neighborhood. Juan knew that Tony went there to visit his family on certain days.

"There it is," Juan said as he pointed towards the building.

"Gustavo, where is my camera? Take pictures immediately." Gustavo clicked away until they were all satisfied. All Juan wanted to do was to get away from the neighbor, so he called Tony to warn him.

Cali tapped Juan's shoulder and he turned. "I know you'll get in touch with him. Warn him that we know where he is right now, and we know where he lives. He's not going anywhere. Try to talk some sense into him and advise him to get my submarine. People that cross me usually die."

The last statement was frostier than ice, but Juan nodded in acknowledgement. He was driven back to the restaurant where he got into his car and drove away, leaving the other group to return to the hell they had come from.

As soon as Juan arrived at Fort Apache, he began to call Tony like a maniac. He left two messages per hour. Juan told Tarzan of the crazy experience and he tried to reach Tony as well. They both knew that Tony would definitely die if he didn't return the money. They were unsure of his life if he did. Cali might be too angry to show him mercy.

Two weeks passed before Tony called Juan back. He was watching the news in his house when his phone buzzed.

"Juan! I hear you've been trying to reach me. Do you miss me that much?"

"WHERE HAVE YOU BEEN?" The anxiety in Juan's voice couldn't be missed.

"Around."

"You know that the entire Cali Cartel wants your head, right? They know where your family is, and they can smoke all of you in seconds."

"I'm fine. Don't you worry. My family is already out of Miami."

"Tony, that man will kill you if he ever sees your face. I am sure of it."

Tony laughed. "You are being too dramatic, Juan. He won't kill me."

"The man I saw will definitely feed you to his dogs without blinking an eye."

Tony stopped laughing. "Was it that terrible?"

"All I can tell you is that you have to disappear. Don't call or text until you are sure that you're too far out of reach."

"Fine."

"Promise me Tony."

"I cross my heart."

Juan had just ended the call when the doorbell rang. His wife walked to the door and tried to open it. Before she could succeed, it was forced open and she was flung against the wall like a racket. Juan's house was suddenly flooded with DEA agents, US marshal and other agencies he couldn't recognize. His children ran down the stairs to find out what the chaos was about, and they joined their parents in raising their hands in surrender. Juan was more embarrassed than he was afraid. He knew that they couldn't find anything in his house. He never allowed intimidating evidence into his house.

After the men had given up on their search, they returned to talk to Juan. He was fuming.

"Oh now you want to talk, huh?"

Special Agent Eaton frowned. "You don't have to sound so testy."

"You raided my house in front of my wife and kids and you think I sound too testy? I can never sound testy enough!"

"We know that you're involved in a submarine deal with a Ludwig Tarzan Fainberg and Tony Yester."

Juan's countenance wouldn't crack, he made sure that he gave nothing away.

"I don't know what you're talking about."

"Of course you don't. No one ever does."

"Are you here to arrest me?"

"No."

"Do you have a warrant?"

The agent's face changed. "We don't have enough evidence, but we will have that in no time."

"Until then, get out of my house."

Once the police agents had cleared out of the house and Juan finally got a minute alone, he called Tarzan.

"Juan?"

"The world is about to come down on us."

CHAPTER 15

When Tarzan was younger, his omens usually came through in the most peculiar way, bedwetting. At first, his mother thought he was doing it on purpose. Then she followed the pattern. He would wet his bed right before he failed test or if someone he knew had been arrested.

As he got older, the bedwetting, graduated to things like sleepwalking, talking loudly in his sleep and nightmares. On the morning of Tarzan's arrest, he woke up on the floor. He was fond of his large king size bed and it took real intent for anyone to fall off the side. When Tarzan found himself with his backside plastered to the cold floor, he knew something terrible was going to happen.

He looked up groggily and found his wife still tucked in, sleeping like a baby. Anyone who saw her would've never guessed that the two had fight so violently the previous night. Lauren had found out that Tarzan had been dating a stripper for a full year and she wanted an explanation that was longer than 'I'm sorry'. She was really pained

"Is it Candy?" she had asked forcefully. "Or maybe it's Anne, your desk girl. The one who particularly works at that front desk in nothing but strings for clothes. Maybe she does double shifts, eh?"

Tarzan had dismissed her claims passively and had told her to go to bed. He easily deflected the conversation telling her that she was being paranoid, and it only fueled her anger. Lauren didn't like to be told that she was crazy. Her mother had been crazy, and it was a very touchy topic for her.

"Call me crazy, but if something else happens, we're done!" she had cried.

"Just make sure you leave my daughter out of this," Tarzan had warned.

"Of course. She's already turning into a female version of you. I won't be surprised if she carries a gun at thirteen."

It only took one slap for Lauren to swallow her next words and go to bed. Tarzan wished he had smacked her much earlier and saved himself all the trouble. The woman was, too much work.

As he dragged his heavy body off the rug, he struggled to stand erect. His left cheek was covered with drool and his right arm felt heavy. He had had a terrible dream where he fought people off, but the memory was too hazy.

Tarzan walked to the bathroom to brush his teeth and take a shower. He stared at his sleepy face. There were rug marks all over his cheeks and his eyes were drooped and bloodshot. He was still a bit hung over for the few bottles he had taken at Porky's the night before. He took out his toothbrush and brushed as hard as he could. He didn't care that his gum was bleeding. He only wanted to get rid of the imminent doom that hung over him like a cloud. It would've helped if he knew what he was supposed to be running from.

He took a quick shower right after brushing the demons out of his teeth. Then he toweled himself down and walked to his room. Lauren was still on the bed, swimming in the white sheets and snoring like a farmer. She had always complained that he snored too much, but she was just as bad. He walked into his closet and found a random shirt and paired it with an Armani jacket. He wasn't supposed to live so luxuriously in order to avoid attention, but all those designer clothes he had bought weren't going to wear themselves.

"Cupcake," he called to his daughter when he was done.

Her room was down the hall and it wasn't likely that she would hear his voice. He took the stairs one at a time, each step much slower than the last. Something was pushing him to run up the stairs, pack up all his belongings and never look back. He knew it would destabilize his daughter. She had just made new friends in her new class and she was happy with life. Tarzan thought it probably had nothing to do with her new friends and more to do with the limousine that brought her to school every day. He also made sure that she wore designer clothing down to her underwear. He loved spending money on her, although he suspected that she wouldn't make real friends. It wasn't a lesson he was willing to teach her yet. He wanted her to enjoy being the queen bee for a while first. She was his baby girl after all, and his girl only deserved to be spoiled.

"Cupcake," he called again and Diana answered.

"Where have you been? I have been calling you," he told her.

There was no trace of anger in his face, but Diana still felt terrible.

"Sorry, papa. Good morning. I was trying to pick between a blue or yellow ribbon," she explained.

She had a yellow ribbon in her hair. He had bought her that ribbon while he was in Russia last year. He liked how it accentuated her eyes. Her mother had bought the blue one. It went without saying that he didn't like it very much.

"So you picked the yellow one. Good girl," he applauded. "Blue is for boys anyway."

"Yes, papa. Blue is for boys."

They took their seats at the dining table and waited for the cook to serve them breakfast. They were egg lovers in the house on some days, they loved Jewish cuisine. Today, they were having *shakshuka* which comprises of egg, tomato sauce, *tofu* and a truckload of spices. Diana wasn't a fan of Jewish meals, but she knew her father took them seriously. It was an abomination to waste food in general, but it was a different level of sin to reject Israeli delicacies. He didn't take it lightly; not even with his wife.

"Thank you Aunty May," Diana grumbled while she pushed her food around in her plate.

"You better finish your food, young lady," he warned her. "How can you not like this?"

"It tastes good, papa," she said as she tried to wipe away thoughts of bacon and sausages that she had eaten at her friend's house after a sleepover.

"It definitely does."

After Tarzan confirmed that his daughter had eaten the last crumb on her plate, he let her take their dishes to the sink. Aunty May usually took care of the dishes, but Tarzan always made sure that Diana took them out. He was not going to raise an overly pampered irresponsible child. His father didn't raise one.

Tarzan had a fleet of cars, and whenever he took Diana to school, he let her pick the car she wanted to take. That morning, he wasn't in the mood to play games with his daughter. He wasn't in the mood for anything in general. He wanted the day to pass with its dark cloud and just be for a while. Tarzan walked purposefully towards the Ferrari and pulled out the keys. Diana tried to catch up with him.

"Daddy, are you okay?" she asked quietly.

"Yes, cupcake. Why wouldn't I be?"

She shrugged as she reached for the door handle. "You look a bit sad. You also didn't play the game today."

"What game?" Tarzan looked clueless.

"I'm supposed to pick the car we're taking. I was going to pick this one anyway," she lied. Tarzan knew she didn't really like the color or the car. Red reminded her of blood, and it scared her.

"You can pick tomorrow," he replied entering the car.

He reached for the seatbelt subconsciously and buckled it. Diana imitated him. The last time she forgot to buckle her seatbelt, she was banished to the back and had to sit there alone. It was the worst. She made sure that it never happened again.

"Okay," she returned. "So will you come instead of Uncle Marty?"

"Yes. Maybe mommy will come."

Diana laughed. "Mommy doesn't have a driver's license. She says that she can't drive without one."

Blood rushed to Tarzan's head in anger. He had told his wife a billion times to apply for a license, but she preferred to procrastinate. Just like everything, he made her so angry.

"How do you even know what a driver's license is? Aren't you in kindergarten?"

Diana mumbled words that he couldn't understand and looked out the window.

Tarzan expertly drove out of his garage and headed straight towards his daughter's school, like any other day. He tuned in to a station he knew that his daughter would love, and she sang along excitedly. It only took seconds for her to forget that they hadn't played their usual game. Before long, the two were holding hands and Tarzan was trying to sing along to the kids ' songs that were playing. It was part of their routine, too.

Tarzan drove slowly all the way to his daughter's school. He wanted the moment to last as long as it could.

"Give papa a kiss, okay?"

Diana obeyed without hesitation. After pecking Tarzan's cheek, she hugged him tightly and placed her cheek on his chest.

"I love you, papa," she said cheerfully.

Those words always drew Tarzan close to tears whenever she said them. She was the only one that could make him feel like jelly.

"I love you too, cupcake. Be good, okay?"

"I will."

Tarzan hugged her tightly and almost forgot to let go.

"Can I go and play with my friends now?" she finally asked. She was getting anxious.

"Of course my darling. You absolutely can."

The little girl ran out of the car like someone was chasing her and made a beeline to the playground. Tarzan chuckled and drove away from the school.

He had barely passed three blocks when he noticed the blue and white cars behind him. They had switched off their siren in order to catch him off-guard. Tarzan wasn't shocked to see them. He knew that day would be strange, and it was best to get past that part of it.

Tarzan drove slowly and allowed the policemen to drive passed him. Once they had overtaken his car, they parked in front of him to block his path.

Special Agent Eaton was the first to approach Tarzan. Tarzan's bear-like appearance might've scared the rest of the team. He suddenly remembered that he hadn't come out with his guns and he was grateful. He might have been arrested for illegal possession of a firearm.

"How may I help you?" Tarzan asked without getting out of his car.

He had to put up the fearless façade although he was deeply afraid. American police and Russians had never been friends or even acquaintances.

"We would like to talk to you in our office."

"What office? Who are you guys?"

A scary thought ran through Tarzan's mind, what if they were the Cali Cartel and they were killing all of Tony's friends one by one? Maybe they had planned to dress like cops. Was Juan still alive?

Agent Eaton stepped forward. "We are from the DEA office downtown."

Tarzan tried to look surprised. "DEA? Am I under arrest? Did you see me with any drugs?"

"No, we are not arresting you Mr. Fainberg."

"Then what do you want?"

"We just want to speak to you briefly."

Tarzan reached for a button to roll his window up. "I'm not going. You can't force me to go."

The man nodded. "You don't want to, but trust me, you have to. It is very crucial." Tarzan decided to take it as an opportunity to make his narrative polished and almost impenetrable.

He knew he was no saint, but he had no idea what they wanted to charge or blackmail him for.

Tarzan agreed to drive behind them to their office and he drove to a tall glassy building. After parking his car, he was led up to a small interrogation room. The room was musky and dark. Tarzan sat quietly in one of the seats waiting to be questioned.

"What do you want to know? I sold nothing. I didn't kill anyone. I didn't even steal from anyone. Why did you bring me here?"

Special Agent Eaton sat across him and looked directly at Tarzan's eyes. He was trying to rattle him, but Tarzan had been in enough staring contests to see through his tricks. He waited until the agent was ready to speak.

"Can you tell us more about your cocaine submarine deal?"

Tarzan froze. His mouth hung open slightly before he recovered and closed his lips.

"I have no idea what you're talking about," he lied.

"We have pictures and thousands of wire taps. We got you," the man said.

"And yet you have refused to arrest me. You know I did nothing wrong."

"We know all about Juan Almeida and Nelson Yester. You're either going home or going to jail," Special Agent stated simply.

"I'm going to need my lawyer."

CHAPTER 16

Juan had decided to put the visit from Cali Cartel and the police behind him. No one had heard that his house was raided, and he was still conducting business as usual. He had managed to purchase a couple of helicopters and spare parts from Moscow for Halifax Company. It was one of his best deals yet. The owner had insisted on coming along to Moscow to see the helicopters himself. Once the deal had been rounded up, Juan ensured that the helicopters would be transported to New York, as he had instructed. The man had other plans.

"I want to visit the synagogue in St. Petersburg," he told Juan. "I assume you already know a few people here who can take me there."

Juan didn't have to think for long. Tarzan's brother lived in Moscow and he was available.

"Just give me a few minutes. You can go to your hotel and freshen up. I will send someone to get you."

"That is perfect. Thank you."

Once the man had left, Juan called Tarzan's brother.

"Taren, I need a quick favor."

Taren sounded very upset, but Juan refused to ask about it. He was more concerned about taking his clients sight-seeing.

"What do you need?"

"I just rounded up with a client here in Moscow and he wants to see the synagogue in St. Petersburg. Could you take him?"

There was a long pause on the other end of the line. Juan thought he might've ended the call.

"Taren?"

"Have you not heard?"

"Heard what?"

"Tarzan had been arrested and now they're on the hunt for you."

Juan froze. He always knew that this time would come. Things were going so well that it was almost unbelievable. Karma had caught up with him.

"When did this happen?" he managed to ask.

Taren's voice was almost as weak as his.

"Yesterday morning. He had just dropped his daughter off at school. I heard Grisha Roizis was the snitch."

Juan had heard the name a couple of times and he had only met him once. The face didn't register in his mind quickly.

"Do you know why he was arrested?"

"I heard it was something about a submarine. You would know better."

Juan definitely knew better. "Thank you, Taren. If you can still help my client, I would really appreciate it."

Juan needed to re-strategize. His entire life and family couldn't be uprooted from Miami. The police would be watching them, and he didn't want to appear as a runner. He knew how bad it would look. He needed to know the charges that had been brought against him. They hadn't stolen a submarine or even bought one. They were only planning on it. There were definitely no charges for attempted purchases; or were there? Juan couldn't tell. The only thing he was sure of, was that he could not go home to Miami. Not yet anyway.

The case was almost like a blur for Tarzan. One second, he was in front of the mean DEA agent assuring him that he had done nothing wrong and the next minute, he was behind bars sitting on a dirty bench trying to sleep. Thoughts of his daughter wouldn't let him have peace. He wondered where she was, what she was doing and what she would think of her father. He had tried to raise her with good morals when he had none.

"Ludwig Fainberg!" Tarzan rushed to the bars. He was glad that help had finally come. His lawyer had gone to sort out his issues and ensure that bail was posted.

The man's face was crestfallen when he returned. His impeccable suit had become rumpled in a few hours. His hair was a mess too.

"I'm really sorry Tarzan."

"It doesn't matter how much the bail costs. I can deal with it," Tarzan assured him.

He had kept the man on the payroll for years especially for that moment. He was glad that he was doing his job. At least, he looked like he was.

"There is no bail. You have to stay here until the trial."

"How is that possible?"

The man shook his head. "They have too much against you, from videos to recordings and countless pictures."

Tarzan was shocked. "How did they get a hold of all these things? There's a rat, isn't there?"

"That is the second thing I came to tell you. Do you know an Alex Yasevich?"

Tarzan laughed bitterly. "That bastard. I knew that radio was a camera and he bugged those stupid phones. You have to tell Juan to get rid of that phone."

"I already did. There is one final thing."

"What?"

"Grisha Roizis bugged Babushka."

"Great."

Galeota didn't grieve when he was informed of Tarzan's arrest. He knew that his boss would be locked away for a long time and he would have to fill his shoes. He had years of practice and he had been the one to turn the club around.

He was having a lot of problems with Kristy. It was not his inability to care for his children or his foul language or even his violence that caused their estrangement. It was his promiscuity. Galeota's line of work exposed him to too many women and it was almost inevitable to fall for them. He still had chemistry with Kristy, but her breasts had fallen, and he was faced with perfect ones on a daily basis.

On countless occasions, he had been caught with various prostitutes. He had even brought one home and Kristy almost burned down the house. The last straw was when she found out that he had been dating a stripper for two full years and she was rumored to be pregnant. She packed her bags, took her kids and left home.

Not long after that Galeota got wind of the police coming for him. He was going to be subpoenaed to testify against Tarzan in court. Galeota was many things, but he wasn't a snitch. Worse still, he wasn't going to lie. He would wait for the air to clear before his return and he would run Porky's for as long as he could.

Galeota bought a ticket for a Caribbean cruise that costed him about two thousand dollars, and he disappeared. When Kristy was asked of his whereabouts, she shrugged.

> "Go and ask his numerous whores. He's probably hiding in someone's basement."

Juan Almeida's arrest was just as dramatic as the scare. Different police officers barged into his house and grabbed him before he could say a word to his wife. Agent Eaton had led the team and he was glad to show Juan the arrest warrant he had brought with him.

"I'm going to read you your rights now."

Juan was thrown into jail, but he came out almost as quickly. He had great lawyers that got him out on bail while he awaited the trial. Unfortunately for the police, the case fell apart since they didn't have pictures of Juan near the submarine and he denied that he was on any of the tapes. There was no solid evidence for any of the counts he was charged with. The court ruled him not guilty for orchestrating the purchase of a thirty five million dollar, Soviet submarine for transporting cocaine. Juan went home like a king.

Tarzan was not as lucky. There were so many pictures of him next to the submarine and Alex Yasevich testified against him. He was found guilty for racketeering, involvement in the purchase of the submarine and was sentenced to nine years in prison.

For the first few weeks, Tarzan's wife visited with beautiful letters from his daughter. He treasured them with all his heart. The sixth and last time she came and informed him that she'll be divorcing him. She would only communicate with him through her lawyers. Tarzan didn't care as long as he still received letters from his daughter. But she didn't write to him.

Every month, Tarzan shriveled away with no one to visit him. Months became years. It was his lowest point.

When Agent Eaton visited Tarzan, he refused to see him. Tarzan knew that the man was up to no good. He was made to sit opposite the man in his jumper and handcuffs. The man wore an awry smile.

"Hello Tarzan. I trust you are doing well," he greeted. The sarcasm was unmistakable.

"What do you want?"

"How long have you been here?"

"Get to the point."

"For thirty months, you have been stuck here for a crime that you did not commit alone. You are paying for other people's sins."

Tarzan had tried not to think of Juan and Tony over the years. None of them had tried to reach out to him.

"Did you come here to tell me to forgive them?"

"Of course not. That's too much for you. I just need you to tell the court what Juan Almeida did."

Tarzan grunted. "And why would I do that?"

"Because you can get out in three months. The only catch is that you can never return to the United States."

Tarzan stood and walked towards the door. "I am not a kid."

Special Agent Eaton returned the following week and Tarzan signed the papers and wrote a perfectly detailed testimony. As the DEA agent had promised, Tarzan was released in three months and taken out of the United States. He chose to go to Panama.

While he was in Panama, he began a small drug trafficking business. Within months, he expanded and included women in his trafficking. It was appalling how easy it was to convince men to sell their daughters for outrageously cheap rates. It was the norm. Tarzan could never give his daughter to a stranger, but he wasn't going to be a preacher. Their gullibility was good for business and he milked it to the last drop.

When Tarzan was finally able to reach out to his lawyer, he only wanted to know about two people.

"How is my girl?"

"She is with her mother. She has a stepfather now."

Tarzan wanted to crush something. "What about Juan?"

“He got forty years. Your testimony cemented everything.”

Tarzan breathed out heavily. “I had to do what I had to do,” he murmured.

“So did Grisha.”

“Send my love.”

“I don’t think he wants it.”

Tarzan hated that his lawyer was chastising him, but the man was right. In the worst situation, everyone was a Grisha. He was not an exception

CHAPTER 17

Running away from influential people like the whole Cali Cartel was only possible when one was rich, and Tony was rich. He knew how to stay well off the radar and still enjoy his newly acquired wealth. It wasn't easy. He had to gather more passports and get rid of the old ones, but it was a small price to pay.

Tony had replayed the conversation with Juan a thousand times. Juan was not as used to bad people as Tony was. He had handled a good number of them in the past. Most times, he has just been lucky, but experience had played a role.

Tony had enjoyed his money so much that he wanted to try his luck with the next payment. He might be able to convince them to pay him the whole thirty million. They could keep the five million for expenses. They weren't receiving the submarine anyway.

In case Juan was right, Tony needed reinforcement. First, he got the contact for one of the Cali Cartel boys. He called and it rang twice before anyone picked up.

"Hello, this is Tony."

"Sorry I didn't get that. What did you say that your name was?"

Tony knew the man was pretending not to hear him. He could tell that he was running. They could already imagine him searching every room for his boss. Eventually, everything calmed down and Tony figured he had found him. The phone was probably on speaker.

"I said this is Tony. I can get you your submarine."

The next voice Tony heard was more family. "Tony I trusted you to keep your hand on the deal, but you disappeared."

"It was a necessary evil, but I have sorted out the little hitch I had. I just need the next payment to show them that we're serious," Tony told him breezily.

"And I will get my submarine?"

"You will get your submarine."

Tony wasn't going to take chances. He had watched the Cali Cartel punish people for swindling them. The culprits never came out alive and they never died quickly. They'll cut a major vein or drown the person in a tub. It was always an awful sight.

Tony didn't want to go in such a humiliating way. He wanted an honorable death.

He collaborated with a cartel that he had previously worked with in Madrid and he recruited six of their men. Each was able-bodied and skilled. He had worked with them and knew of their potential. With new confidence, Tony called the number again.

"I just flew into Barcelona," he said in a rushed tone. He wanted to sound exhausted and in a hurry. "I will take a train to Madrid from Barcelona and meet you at the train station. Is that fine?"

The man didn't run this time. "It's definitely fine. We'll be there to pick you up once your train arrives."

"Thank you. Can I still call this number, or is there another number I should call when I arrive?"

"This one is fine," the man said and the call ended.

Tony had to applaud him for his calmness. If someone had stolen ten million dollars from him or his boss, he wouldn't be so calm and collected. He would've lost his cool after the first ten seconds.

Tony Yester sat in his rented car at the Madrid train station an hour before the train from Barcelona arrived. The other men had taken their positions in the station watching vigilantly and awaiting a situation that would require them to take action. They hid in plain sight as planned. One sat on a bench with a book in his hand. The other was walking with a phone to his ear. Tony Yester could not see the other four, but he could hear them. They all had earpieces to communicate with each other.

At the exact arrival time, the train from Barcelona stopped and everyone rushed out of the train. Some walked while others called taxis. Tony waited for the buzz to die down a little. Once he was ready, he called the number again.

"Hello?"

"Where are you?"

The buzz around them made it easy to lie. "I'm at the train station. I just arrived. Where are you?"

"I'm at the train station, too. Where can we meet?"

Tony looked around and spotted a taxi on the other side of the road. There was a man in front in a white shirt. Tony was wearing a black polo with a black jacket over it.

"I'm in a taxi," he said. "I'm wearing a white shirt. Can you see me?"

"Yes, I can."

Suddenly, three men appeared out of nowhere. One pointed a gun at the confused man in the front seat while the other aimed at the driver. Three of them jumped in the back seat and ordered the driver to move. A jeep followed them closely until they disappeared.

Tony shook his head and dispatched his men. He drove away from the scene as quickly as he could manage and returned to his makeshift apartment. After fifteen minutes, he called the number again.

The voice on the other end sounded rushed.

"We didn't see you. Where were you?"

"I was at the train station, but you didn't show up," Tony told them.

"We were there, but we can always come back to get you. It won't take long," he promised.

Tony laughed. "Tell your boss that you missed your chance. I was there, but you couldn't find me."

"Fuck you."

Tony laughed again. "Tell your man that I have his ten million dollars and he can't do anything about it."

"He is going to kill you."

"Then I better hurry and squander this beautiful money before I die."

The line went dead. Tony knew that he had to disappear as soon as possible. Cali was known internationally, and they could catch him anywhere. He had to think of a continent that they couldn't infiltrate or have no desire to.

There was only one place he had in his mind.

CHAPTER 18

Tarzan had only been in Panama for a few months before he got arrested. He had been in prison in Florida for three years. One would think that he would be used to losing his freedom, but the experience was much worse than the first time. He was seized with a ton of cocaine in his possession. Someone had snitched on him again. There was another Grisha Roizis in his life.

> "Gregory never seems to get away from me," he had murmured as one of the cops threw him on the ground and slapped handcuffs against his wrist.

There was no way out of it.

There was no trial and Tarzan was not allowed to make contact with anyone outside the prison. It seemed like a normal occurrence as the other inmates were used to the maltreatment they received. Every day, they were taken out in the sun to work on the farms. Tarzan began to look forward to the days in the sun. It reminded him of his random trips to different countries on Juan's plane. He missed Juan.

Tarzan's reputation preceded him in the prison. The prison guards found out that he was a major drug and human trafficker for years and they had more to gain from him. In due time, he became a consultant. He would advise the fastest most efficient ways to sell their products. Including locations to find women who were willing to work in other countries at meagre prices. Tarzan was like a God in the prison, but it wasn't enough for him. He knew he would never be able to return to the United States since he was banned, but he missed the sand and the water. He wished to go back to Florida.

CHAPTER 19

Tarzan had only been visited once. There was a filmmaker who wanted to make a movie about his story. At first, Tarzan wasn't excited about the plan, but he figured that it was harmless. If he wanted a story, he could get a story, as long as he wasn't working with the police.

Before the filmmaker arrived, Tarzan had received more threats than he had in a lifetime. The Cali Cartel had heard about the filmmaker all the way from Columbia. They were going to slaughter Tarzan if he said a word to him. Then they would take his daughter and sell her to the dogs. Tarzan's wife had been taking care of her while he was in prison, but he knew it would be easy to get the girl out of her hands. She barely cared about her.

Once the filmmaker arrived, Tarzan had to sense him off. His daughter was more important than any blockbuster movie. His daughter was more important than the world and he would never let a hair on her head go missing. He could stay in prison forever as long as she was safe. However, he wanted to get out no matter what it took.

It was a mere conversation with one of the prison guards that gave Tarzan a bright idea. Tarzan had begun to treasure the time they spent under the sun more than anything. He had been given a private cell out of the respect they had for him. He had also received a few 'relief materials 'from the prison guards he had helped. Even the prisoners showed loyalty.

One afternoon, he was working on his own portion of the farm although they had told him that he could stay back. He was a VIP prisoner. A guard wanted to talk with him while he worked.

"I will just tell you the truth. Everyone else comes to you for advice on how to move cocaine and drugs, but-"

"They do? I had no idea." Tarzan was always on his toes. He was done with trusting everyone. There were snitches everywhere.

" You don't have to pretend. I'm not here to catch you in the act of anything. I just need you to mentor me," he said. Tarzan carried a bundle of weeds and walked to the heap to dump it.

"What do you need from me?"

"I am in love with someone," he said.

"I..."

The man hushed him. "Everyone here knows that you are good with women. I am not. I just need a few pointers."

Tarzan smiled. It had been a while since he talked about anything that was not a crime.

"Who is she?"

"Sabrina."

Tarzan was confused. He had no idea who the man was talking about.

"You know Sabrina," he said. "The woman that brings the cigarettes and everything."

The smuggler. Of course. Tarzan had never spoken to her directly, but he was always offered her products. He had refused cocaine so many times, but her cigarettes were quality.

"The woman that smuggles cigarettes to this place?"

The prison guard walked closer to Tarzan and lowered his voice.

"She smuggles everything from cigarettes, good old mama's cooking to phones."

"Phones?"

"Yes. You need one?"

Tarzan scratched his head. "Well... yes, but I need something more. Can she bring a kid into this place? I would love to see my daughter."

The man looked pitiful for a second. "I have little girl too. I'm really sorry that you have not seen yours."

"Thank you."

"I will tell you something. If you can convince her to spend a night with me, then I will help her get your daughter to you."

Tarzan could not believe his luck. He found Sabrina the next day while she was peddling small tablets to prisoners. They were definitely not acetaminophen as they claimed, but he did not probe.

"I have a business deal for you," he said simply.

"Oh you're Tarzan. I've heard of you. What can I help you with?"

Tarzan smiled. "How rich do you want to be?"

He did not need an answer because the woman was grinning from ear to ear.

The next morning, the prison guard arrived in Tarzan's cell with the biggest grin. He could not contain his joy and he wanted to share it with someone.

"What did you tell her?" he asked Tarzan.

"Who?"

"Don't joke with me. She was all over me only a day after we had that conversation. She had never noticed me before then."

Tarzan shrugged. "You asked for a favor and I did it. It wasn't a big deal."

The prison guard walked to Tarzan's bench and sat comfortably. Tarzan wasn't interested in the kiss and tell story the man was about to tell, but he had to bear it.

"She was the best sex of my life. I knew with that strut that she had something in her," he rambled.

"I'm happy for you!"

"She knew everything I wanted without even asking her. She touched me everywhere and I literally had to pry her off of me."

Tarzan knew why she had been so good. He had told her that her pay depended on how satisfied he was.

Tarzan nodded. "Good for you."

"Now I know I owe you a whole lot. For sex that was better than my wife's, I'm willing to pay anything."

Tarzan nodded. "Good. May I talk to Sabrina in private, then?"

"That's it?"

"For now."

"Thirty minutes."

Just as the prison guard promised, Sabrina was in his cell in thirty minutes. She was dressed in a plain gown and there was a scarf covering her hair. Tarzan did not find her attractive in any way. She walked into the cell and the door closed behind her.

"When will I get my money?"

Tarzan reached under his pillow and pulled out a hundred dollar note.

"This should be enough."

The woman had not seen that much money in a while.

"It is," she answered courteously although she wanted to squeal. No one ever gave her that much for sex.

"I hear you can smuggle anything into this place."

She nodded repeatedly. "Yes, I can."

"Can you bring a human being into this place?"

The woman seemed to think about it briefly.

"A child will be easy, but an adult is more complicated."

Tarzan nodded. "So if you can get someone in, then you can definitely get the person out."

"Yes."

"What if I save you one of those trips and I pay you a thousand times the money in your hand."

It took Sabrina a while to catch on, but once she did, she gasped.

"You want me to get you out for a hundred thousand dollars."

Tarzan nodded. "Can you?"

The prison guard was upset that for the next few days, all Tarzan wanted to do was talk to Sabrina. He had become jealous of them and he often wondered what they did. Everyone else wondered, too. They had even started calling her Tarzan's whore, but she never got upset. She had a lot more to gain. She refused to succumb to name calling.

The prison guard was so perturbed that he formed a habit of following Sabrina to Tarzan's cell. He would stand outside and try to listen to the two. Tarzan was too smart to say anything loudly except words that were not incriminating. Sometimes he would form fake scripted conversations and write Sabrina's replies so they could play along. The guard was satisfied with this. At least, no one was moaning.

Tarzan convinced Sabrina to have sex with the guard the night before the plan would be executed. She thought it would be better on the day of their escape just before his shift was over. She was right. He took her to the most bearable toilet in the prison which the guards used. After she had faked two or three orgasms, he was star struck. She told him she wanted to speak with Tarzan alone and he let her. She had come with a bag full of heavy cooking supplies. There was a big pot that was used to fit everything. She emptied them in Tarzan's cell and squeezed him into the pot. The bag was slightly heavier than it was when she came in. As she dragged the bag out, the guard helped her with it. Tarzan tried his best to play dead and restrict his movements.

"Why do you always go there to see Tarzan?" he asked her.

"Are you jealous?"

He shrugged. "Yes. I know I have a wife, but I am jealous."

Sabrina touched his chest seductively and looked right into his eyes.

"You don't have to be."

"What do you two do together?"

"I told him that I can't bring his daughter to him. Now he makes me come in to pray for him every day. He says that I must repeat everything in the synagogue once I get there."

The prison guard paused. "Are you Jewish?"

"No but he looked so pathetic that I pretended to be."

The prison guard owned a truck. He lifted her bag into the trunk and went around to the driver's side.

"They will seize my kitchen supplies if they see them in your truck," she said.

The man paused. She was right. He had to be smart about his exit. He would get into trouble, too if he was caught with her at the gate. There was only one way out.

The two carried the big bag to the seat and bent it over. One of the rags in the truck served as a cover for the bag and it blended easily with the sheets. Once they were satisfied, the guard drove towards the gate.

"Gerard." The military man at the gate had never been a fan of Gerard's and he never hid his dislike.

"My shift is over."

"But you just got here." The hostile undertone could not be missed. "Who is the girl?"

"She helps with the cooking for the prisoners," Gerard replied. It was difficult to hold back.

"Does she cook for you too?"

Sabrina, who was a natural born actress began to act agitated. "I'm really sorry to interrupt this conversation, but someone just informed me that my sister is in the hospital and she is bleeding to death?"

"Hit and run?"

"No. It was an attempted abortion."

The military man looked disgusted. "If you're not careful, you will end up like her."

"Please just let me go and see her."

"Get out of here," he said and opened the gate for them.

As they drove past, Gerard turned to Sabrina. "How is your sister? I hope we can get to her in time."

Sabrina laughed aloud. "There is no sister!"

Gerard joined her in laughing, but his heart was troubled. She was such a great actress there that he wondered what else she had lied about.

Tarzan who was still squashed in a pot and struggling to breathe stayed quiet as they had planned. The man girdle had been snapped. He only had one left.

Sabrina insisted that Gerard should drive her home. She had no home, but her friend agreed to let her use her home for a few days. Gerard carried the pot with her to the kitchen. When she dropped it, the cover opened slightly, and Tarzan's jumper could be seen.

"What was that?" he asked suddenly alarmed. He reached for the pot cover, but Sabrina stopped him.

"I've been stealing some old coveralls from the prison for a while. I just wanted to make clothes for children that have none. See?"

She opened the pot slightly and the orange overall was visible again. "That is why I lied to the man at the gate. I couldn't get caught."

"Why didn't you ask me? I could have gotten you more. You're so adorable."

Sabrina smiled. "I know. Now can I take you to heaven?" she asked as she led him towards her friend's bedroom.

While she desecrated a matrimonial bed, Tarzan ran for his life.

As Tarzan had promised, he reached out to his lawyer and Sabrina was paid before the week ran out. She disappeared afterwards. Tarzan found his way out of Panama and into Costa Rica. Afterwards, he moved to Cuba before he eventually ended up in Moscow. With the help of his old friends, he got his Russian passport reinstated and he was repatriated by the Russian government. They had claimed that it was wrong for their citizen to be imprisoned without a proper trial. The Panama government accepted it in good faith claiming that they would have deported him anyway. Gerard however was arrested and thrown into the same jail. He cursed the day that he had spoken to Tarzan.

Once Tarzan was able to reunite with his daughter in Moscow, he withdrew the testimony he had made against Juan Almeida. Since they had nothing against Juan, he was released from prison.

Tarzan met a Canadian woman in Moscow who fell in love with him. He had never been known to reject women and with her connections, he thought it was wise to marry her. While in Moscow, he worked with a few drug traffickers as a 'problem solver'. It didn't pay as much, but it was good enough for him. Although he did not say it often, he missed Miami.

One morning, while he reminisced on his balcony, he remembered the filmmaker. He still kept the blackberry he had used in the prison. Once he found it, he searched for the man's email address and sent him a brief email. It was finally time to make that movie.

Tony Yester was never caught. Until...

EPILOGUE

Tiller Russell had developed a new chant to keep him sane during his journey.

I'm going to make the world's greatest movie.

I'm going to blow minds away.

I'm going to make a truckload of money from this.

The 'short poem' had taken him all the way from Miami to South Africa. It had led him through some strange streets even when people constrained him while he pretended not to notice. It had led him to a shabby hotel on the outskirts of the city. It had brought him to the hotel he was instructed to go to.

A lot of people would label Tiller Russell as crazy and it wasn't farfetched. Ever since a DEA agent had told him of a trio that almost succeeded in selling a submarine to a drug lord. One had made away with the money while the other two had taken the fall. Russell had listened to every side of the story except the most important side; the one who had made away with all the money.

It was impossible to take hold of the man. Juan Almeida and Tarzan Fainberg had spoken to Tiller Russell with little cajoling. Each laughed when he hinted that he'd like to talk to Tony Yester. It was hilarious to them that he would even consider it. Russell ignored all their jeering and searched. He sent out messages to all the people who he suspected would be privy to information about Tony's whereabouts.

The best day of Russell's life was the day that Tony Yester reached out to him. He was on set, still working on the Odessa story when his phone beeped. He was not used to reading messages from strangers, but ever since his bounty hunt for Tony Yester started, he was always quick to grab his phone. When he read the message, he laughed aloud.

You have met the waiters. You can come and meet the chef.

Russell laughed aloud and grabbed his jacket.

"Is there a problem, sir?" one of his assistants asked.

"Of course not."

"The filming session for the day isn't over," the man said to him in dragged words like he had lost his mind.

"I know that. Tell my assistant to roundup. I will call her when I'm done "

There were instructions that followed subsequently. He always had a small overnight bag in his car for emergency travelling. Once he received instructions to go to the airport, he withdrew a lot of cash and did so. The next step was to buy a ticket to a city he could not pronounce. All he knew was that it was in East Africa.

When he arrived, he received the next step of instructions. There was a hotel on the other side of the city. The address was sent via text and he was instructed to delete it on arrival. Russell did not receive any other messages that night. The next morning, his phone rang. He didn't recognize the number, but he was positive that it belonged to Tony Yester. He was right.

"Downstairs. Five minutes Porsche Cayenne," the voice on the other end said.

The accent was just as thick as Russell would have expected. He took a three-minute shower and rushed downstairs. Once he reached the ground floor, he walked through a hotel lobby where he found a couple of tall well-built men in Armani suits. They looked nothing like business travelers or tourists. Russell knew that he had come to the right place.

He walked outside and found the Porsche Cayenne as he was told. The driver was so unexpected. He wore dark sunglasses and invited Russell to sit. Once he was in, the man drove off at a hundred miles per hour until he had reached an abandoned path. Russell was almost sure that he was close to meeting his fate. As he stared out the window and tried to distract himself, Tony Yester slapped him across his chest.

"Ouch!"

"You better be who the fuck you say you are and this better be what the fuck you say it is!"

"I swear I am a filmmaker. You could have checked me out on the internet."

"I did. You wouldn't be here otherwise."

"I swear I am here to make a movie. That is all."

"It better be. If not, we are going to have a very big problem."

When Tony Yester finally parked his car, they were on an airstrip. There were three helicopters lined up. Tony Yester led him to one of them. Once they were settled, Tony urged him to start the interview.

"Ask me."

"So I need to understand. Where do you fit in the power structure of Medellin Cartel?"

Tony Yester was silent for a full minute. It was obvious that Russell had caught him off-guard and he had no plans of answering such an intrusive question.

"You're fucking curious, eh? Just leave it like that. Let us not mention those things."

Russell moved on to the next question. He did not want to upset Tony and end the interview prematurely.

"Did they ever stop looking for the ten million dollars?"

"All I can tell you is that all my enemies are dead and I'm going to see them in fucking hell when I arrive there."

"Were you ever going to give Juan Almeida or Tarzan Fainberg any money?"

Tony smiled. "I was ready to give them a million dollars at first. Then, I started spending the millions, and I changed my mind. I would just give them five hundred thousand dollars. Then..."

"Then...?"

"Then Tarzan flipped on all of us and made the decision easier. I was not going to give my money to a fucking rat."

LATER...

Turns out that Tony had been "hiding out" in South Africa with his Italian girlfriend for fourteen years and was arrested in December 2017 when visiting Rome, Italy. He had been extradited to the United States in July 2019 where he faced a life sentence for imposing on the world of international narcotics trafficking.

Tony showed the director his Russian fighter jet, which had five million in the cockpit, which was the fugitive's getaway plan, and then told his side of the story.

United States Attorney Maria Chapa Lopez announces the unsealing of a 2017 indictment charging Nelson Pablo Yester-Garrido (62, Cuba) with conspiracy to distribute large amounts of high-grade marijuana and possessing a firearm in furtherance of that conspiracy. If convicted on all counts, Yester-Garrido faces a maximum penalty of life in federal prison.

According to court documents, from the late 1980s through early 1997, Yester-Garrido was part of a group involved in importing kilogram amounts of cocaine and other narcotics into the United States, including by negotiating the purchase of a Russian diesel submarine for Colombian drug suppliers. According to law enforcement, around 1997, Yester-Garrido fled to South Africa to escape prosecution related to charges filed in the Southern District of Florida (which have since been dismissed).

In January 2015, the DEA began investigating Yester-Garrido and several other Florida-based individuals who were distributing large amounts of high-grade marijuana to individuals and groups in central Florida. In January 2017, an indictment was returned in the Middle District of Florida charging three of Yester-Garrido's co-conspirators (Juan Almeida, Andrew Cassara, and Wade Jones, Jr.) with conspiracy to distribute marijuana. In 2018, Almeida, Cassara, and Jones were sentenced to varying terms of imprisonment.

In October 2017, a grand jury in the Middle District of Florida returned an indictment charging Yester-Garrido with conspiracy to possess with the intent to distribute marijuana and possessing a firearm in furtherance of a drug trafficking crime. Later that month, based upon a provisional arrest warrant requested by the U.S. government, Italian authorities apprehended Yester-Garrido at the Fiumicino Airport in Rome, Italy. In July 2019, the Italian judicial authorities and